Drafting with AutoCAD

Peter Ingham

BUTTERWORTH HEINEMANN

Newnes
An imprint of Butterworth-Heinemann Ltd
Linacre House, Jordan Hill, Oxford OX2 8DP

 PART OF REED INTERNATIONAL BOOKS

OXFORD   LONDON   GUILDFORD   BOSTON
MUNICH   NEW DELHI   SINGAPORE   SYDNEY
TOKYO   TORONTO   WELLINGTON

First published 1991

British Library Cataloguing in Publication Data
Ingham, P. C.
  Drafting with AutoCAD.
  1. Technical drawings, use of computers
  I. Title
  604.2402854

ISBN 0 7506 0073 X

Typeset by BP Integraphics Ltd, Bath, Avon
Printed and bound in Great Britain by Thomson Litho, East Kilbride

Contents

Contents

Preface

It is commonly claimed that computer aided drafting, in addition to its other benefits, provides a means for the rapid production of good quality engineering drawings. In practice, it is often found that the drawings produced fall short of those obtained by more traditional means in their clarity of communication. In computer aided drafting, as in other computer applications, if the full potential of the system is to be achieved, there should be a partnership between human and machine with each making full and complementary use of their own special talents.

It is unreasonable to expect that the adoption of computer aided methods should by itself result in the production of good quality engineering communication. Using a word-processor does not guarantee a lucid report even though the grosser errors can be eliminated with spelling checkers, thesauri and stylistic analysers. Similarly, with drafting systems it is not enough to produce drawings with neat text and lines of consistent thickness if the form and size information is difficult to abstract quickly and unambiguously.

It is, then, important not just to attain proficiency in the use of a drafting system but to study also the principles of engineering graphics. These have evolved over many years and are formalized in national standards by all industrialized countries. Fortunately, particularly for younger engineers, there is a current tendency for these national standards to converge.

AutoCAD is by far the most widely used of the many drafting systems now available – over 200,000 copies have been sold world-wide with almost a third being sold in Europe – and because of the wide variety of its commands, it is an excellent choice for teaching purposes. Apart from its own virtues, it has had a profound influence on the development of computer aided drafting systems in general. Most engineering courses now include a treatment of computer aided drafting, which is often taught in conjunction with general engineering graphics. This text is based on the premise that these two aspects of engineering communication – computer engineering drafting and engineering graphics principles – are indivisible and should be learned together.

The book is organized into sections, each of which broadly deals with some aspect of practical engineering drafting. Although there is a logical progression through the principles of AutoCAD and basic engineering drafting, readers are encouraged to anticipate future material by experimentation using the excellent AutoCAD **HELP** facility. This process of 'discovery, then consolidation' is a most efficient way of learning any computer system.

Chapter 1 is a short introduction to the operating environment – the hardware and systems software used with AutoCAD.

Chapter 2 describes the basic principles of AutoCAD.

Chapter 3 is an introduction to the drafting standards which are applicable to computer aided drafting.

Chapter 4 describes the action and use of the AutoCAD drawing editor.

Chapter 5 details the AutoCAD grid and snap facilities which are necessary for rapid drafting.

Chapter 6 augments previous discussion of the elements used to create a drawing.

Chapters 7 and 8 are treatments of the extensive range of AutoCAD's editing commands.

Chapter 9 explains how drawings can be organized into layers and how standardization can be encouraged by the use of layer schedules.

Chapter 10 details the use of text styles and how text can be used to annotate drawings clearly.

Chapter 11 is a description of standard dimensioning and tolerancing practice and how AutoCAD can be used to provide clear form and size information.

Chapter 12 shows how the appearance of drawings can be improved by the use of polylines to create different line thicknesses and how isometrics and sketches can be done in AutoCAD.

Chapter 13 explains the use of blocks and attributes and how they can improve drawing throughput.

Chapter 14 is a treatment of drawing communication. It describes how good plots can be obtained and how drawings can be transferred between systems.

Appendix A contains examples of standard conventions and abbreviations used in engineering drawing and also details of the standard tolerance frames used widely in many countries.

Appendix B is a useful index of AutoCAD commands and the menu items in which they can be found. This should be useful to system 'browsers'. A list of handy system variables is also given.

I am grateful to the staff of Autodesk (UK) Ltd whom I found to be most helpful and encouraging.

P.C.I.

Note

AutoCAD, AutoLisp and AutoSolid are registered trademarks of Autodesk Inc.
CP/M is a registered trademark of Digital Research.
Deskjet and Laserjet are registered trademarks of Hewlett Packard.
MS-DOS and OS/2 are registered trademarks of the Microsoft Corporation.
Unix is a registered trademark of the AT & T Company.

1 Introduction

A discussion of drafting systems, the environment in which they run and the hardware that they use.

Drafting systems

Of the many drafting systems commercially available, AutoCAD is probably the most versatile. In contrast to other systems, it offers a broad range of facilities which can be used in many application areas to produce component drawings, schematics, layouts and presentation displays. AutoCAD differs also from many other systems in its open nature; it can be modified easily to suit a particular field. These two qualities – breadth of facilities and adaptability – carry with them an attendant problem, however. AutoCAD has a very large repertoire of commands which may be confusing to new users. In practice, however, most experienced operators do not use all the available facilities regularly; they develop with practice a working subset that suits their specialized needs and methods of working. AutoCAD is particularly good in its capability for allowing users to choose different ways of working.

Over the last few years, computerized drafting systems have supplanted manual drafting in many areas. This is due to their offering many clear benefits. Their main advantage is that they have the potential for improving engineering communication. Used correctly, they can create clear and accurate drawings to a consistent standard. It must be admitted, though, that the use of a drafting system does not guarantee good drawings; drafters must still be trained in the craft of technical drawing in order to take advantage of the full possibilities offered.

In the right conditions, drafting systems can also increase drawing throughput appreciably. In many engineering environments, it is common for new drawings to be created by modifying old drawings. This can be done rapidly and cleanly using computerized systems. Most drawings contain standard symbols and conventions. AutoCAD, like other systems, allows these to be stored away and recalled at will with very little time and effort. It is also possible to store drawings, or parts of drawings, so that they can be used with variations of dimension and form. In an extreme case, producing a full drawing can be reduced to the clerical exercise of typing the variant dimensions. Fortunately for drafters, this is rare.

In order to define an engineering component, the bald details of its geometric form are insufficient; it is also necessary to hold details of other attributes such as the material of which it is made, its surface finish and how it is to be manufactured. These are usually added to the conventional drawing as annotation. AutoCAD can hold them in a much more useful and formalized way as part of the drawing definition file. The file can then be processed to produce costings, bills of quantities and reports.

Since a drawing is held on the computer in a form which is precise and unambiguous, the details of a component can be passed on to a wide variety of other systems such as computer aided manufacture, finite element analysis and desk top publishing. There are many systems which allow communication with AutoCAD and its drawing definition format **DXF** (Drawing Interchange File) has become a widely used standard. In addition, AutoCAD supports drawing interchange via **IGES** (Initial Graphics Exchange Specification) files.

Because of these and other benefits, it is not surprising that the use of computerized drafting systems has become commonplace in engineering.

Hardware

There are many variants of computer system that can be used to run AutoCAD and it would be inappropriate to discuss all the possibilities here. We shall just deal with the most commonly found configurations.

You are most likely running your AutoCAD on a microcomputer. This may stand alone or be connected to other computers through a network. The conventional system consists of:

- A **processor**, which carries out the instructions of the program.
- A **keyboard**, through which commands and the data on which they act are passed to the processor.
- A **video display**, which enables the computer to communicate with the operator.
- **Short term store**, which is a kind of scratchpad into which programs and data are loaded and run.
- **Long term store**, which may be of two kinds: the hard disk contains programs and data which are commonly needed and so is rapidly accessed but of limited capacity, the floppy disk is slower but is used to hold bulk information.
- A **printer**, which provides a record on paper of computer output.

For graphics use, this basic system will be augmented in various ways.

Despite external appearances, graphics systems involve a lot of numerical calculation and they are usually run interactively. In such applications, it is essential that operation should be as fast as possible in order to permit the human partner to work effectively. The normal processor may be assisted in its calculations by a **maths co-processor** which considerably speeds up the action. Since the co-processor is located in the same box as the normal processor, users may be unaware of its presence; they would certainly be aware of its absence.

Since the operator is creating pictures, it is necessary that a **graphics display** should be provided. This may be in addition to the text display, so that the user can enter and receive words on one display while operating on and seeing graphics on another display. It is more usual, nowadays, for a single display to be used for both purposes. In order to show pictures, a special screen must be used and a graphics card will be installed inside the system. This is a device which produces the display: there are many proprietary graphics cards supporting different display resolutions and displayable colours. AutoCAD can handle a wide range of them. It is likely that you will be using a display with at least 640 dots in the horizontal direction and 350 in the vertical with at least 16 simultaneously displayable different colours.

You will also have some **graphics input device**: a mouse or a digitizing tablet. Items on the graphics display can be referred to by moving a crosshair cursor to the appropriate position and depressing a button on the input device. The movement of the input device is followed on the screen by movement of the crosshair cursor. In addition to pointing to objects or positions on the screen, you can also enter commands to the system by pointing to commands in a displayed list called a 'menu'. There is also a menu card, supplied with the system, which is partitioned into areas corresponding with AutoCAD commands. If this is mounted on a flat board called a 'graphics tablet' and you move the graphics input device to one of these areas and depress a button, then the relevant command will be communicated to the system. AutoCAD input is particularly flexible and will be dealt with in more detail later.

When you have created a drawing, it may be stored as a named file on the computer storage device and may be retrieved for display and editing on the screen. In most environments, it is still necessary to create drawings on paper for recording and discussion purposes and this may be done in two ways. A drawing may be plotted on a specialized **plotter**. There are several types, the most common being pen plotters and electrostatic plotters. Alternatively, a coarser kind of drawing can be produced on an appropriate type of printer. The drawings in this book were mainly produced on a Hewlett Packard Deskjet printer.

Software – the operating system

It is very likely that, when you power up your computer and start to use AutoCAD, you will see a prompt appear on the screen – 'C>', for example. You may then respond by typing a series of commands that result in the AutoCAD program being performed. In order to provide the correct conditions for AutoCAD to run, you have been using another piece of software called 'the operating system'.

The operating system

This is a suite of software which is supplied with the system and which helps the user to run applications programs easily and assists in all the necessary housekeeping tasks, such as storing security copies of drawing files. There are several common operating systems, the type depending to a great extent on the computer that you are using. Each of these presents the user with a different interface to the computer hardware. Some examples of operating systems are MS-DOS, PC-DOS, CP/M, Unix and OS/2. It is not appropriate to describe all of these in detail here; instead, we shall give a brief account of the one that is probably the most popular currently. This is MS-DOS. Only the facilities that are of immediate use in running AutoCAD will be described and you can be sure that all of these facilities will be provided by any other operating system that you might use.

Files

Files are of various kinds, the most obvious distinction being between files that would be readable to a human being if they were printed and those which would not. A name and address file, as used in a mailing program, would very probably be fairly intelligible if printed out. The AutoCAD program would, if printed, be a jumble of nonsense. Files are given names – in MS-DOS these can be up to eight characters long – and it is good practice, even with such a short name length, to make a file's name as self-descriptive as possible.

A filename can also have an 'extension', up to three characters long, after the filename and separated from it by a full stop. The extension is often used to describe the type of file and there are some standard extensions in MS-DOS: EXE, COM, SYS and BAT are some of these. The extension that will immediately concern you is DWG; this is the extension that is used in AutoCAD to show that a file is a drawing file. Thus, a drawing file might be christened 'BRAKE276.DWG'. If your installation uses a drawing register, then the file name might be just the drawing number. When filenames are used in some MS-DOS commands, it is sometimes convenient to show, not one file, but a group of files. This is done by using '*', the 'wildcard' character which represents zero or more unspecified characters. Thus, all the drawing files might be nominated by '*.DWG'.

Directories

Files – both programs and data – will probably be stored on a hard disk on your system. The hard disk is conventionally referred to as Drive C in MS-DOS, and, in commands, 'C:'. The floppy disk, similarly, is called 'A:' (and, if you have a twin floppy system, the second drive is called 'B:'). At a given time, one of the drives will be the current drive and this is shown, for convenience and safety, in the operating system prompt as 'C>'or 'A>'. You can make other drives current by typing their names in response to the

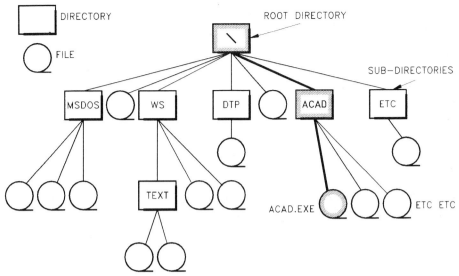

Figure 1.1 Directory

prompt. If drive C were current and we wished to change to drive A, then the following command would serve:

C>**A:**
A>

Note that in this example, as in those that follow, the user input is shown in boldface print.

It is possible that your hard disk might be partitioned into several logical disks; for instance, part might be referred to as drive C and part as drive D.

Details of files on a disk are held in indexes called 'directories' which are analogous to the contents lists of books. Unlike a list of contents, however, a directory can hold details of other directories. At any time, you will be logged into one directory on one drive; you will then have access to all the files to which it refers. If you want to find out the details of all the files on your working directory, then you use the command **DIR**. A list of all the files contained in the directory will then be displayed. It is common for directories to hold many files and if you use **DIR** to list them, then they will scroll upwards so quickly that you will be unable to read them. You can add the option **/P** to the **DIR** command and this will display the files one screenful at a time, progress from one screenful to another being made by typing any character. If you wished to list the files on the floppy drive A, and the current drive was C, then the following command sequence would be suitable:

C>**A:**
A>**DIR /P**

Since directories can hold details of other directories, the directory structure will be tree-like – Figure 1.1 shows an example. Notice that the name ACAD has been used for both a directory and a file. This is quite common and causes no confusion. It is usual to give a file an extension, in contrast to a directory which commonly has none. Thus, we refer to 'the directory

ACAD' and 'the files ACAD.EXE and ACAD.OVL'. The directory at the top is, oddly enough, called the 'root directory' and has a special name, '\'. This backslash character must not be confused with '/' which we used earlier in front of the option in the command **DIR**. We can move up and down in directory trees by using 'pathnames'. If we wished to display the contents of the directory ACAD in Figure 1.1, then we could use the following commands:

> C > **CD \CAD**
> C > **DIR /P**

If the current directory were already the root directory, then it would be unnecessary to use the symbol '\'. **CD ACAD** would suffice.

More about files

The full identification of a file is given by its detailed pathname. For instance, the full pathname of the AutoCAD program in Figure 1.1 is 'C:\ACAD\ACAD.EXE'. This is composed of the following elements:

C: Drive C (the hard disk)

on which is

\ the root directory,

which has a sub-directory

ACAD

which contains the file

ACAD.EXE

in which we are interested.

There are several commands which can be used outside AutoCAD to manipulate files. For instance, it is likely that you will be keeping your drawings on floppy disks rather than filling the limited storage space on the hard disk with them. You can copy files from the hard disk to a floppy disk by using the **COPY** command. If you are in the directory ACAD and you wish to copy the drawing DRAWING.DWG to a floppy disk, then, after posting your target disk in the floppy drive, you can type:

COPY C:\ACAD\DRAWING.DWG A:

or

COPY DRAWING.DWG A:

since you are in ACAD already.

If you have second thoughts about the name of the file and consider it insufficiently descriptive, then you can rename it by:

COPY DRAWING.DWG A:BRAKE276.DWG

Or, you can change its name after copying it by:

COPY DRAWING.DWG A:
RENAME A:\DRAWING.DWG A:\BRAKE276.DWG

After copying the drawing file to the floppy disk, you can get rid of it from the hard disk by:

ERASE C:\ACAD\DRAWING.DWG

or

ERASE DRAWING.DWG

since you are still in the ACAD directory.

Although the second, abbreviated command is perfectly legal, you are advised to use the full pathname if you are not fully familiar with MS-DOS. This will ensure that you do not remove the wrong file. Similarly, it is best to avoid the use of wildcards when you are new to the system since their misuse can lead to disaster.

Before storing anything on a floppy disk, it must be prepared for use (or 'formated'). This is done by using the command:

FORMAT A:

This has been a very quick introduction to some of the commands in MS-DOS. Although most of the operations described can be done inside AutoCAD, it is advisable to find out more about MS-DOS as soon as you can. The manuals that come with the system are usually quite readable.

Summary

- The hard disk is usually drive C.
- The floppy disk is usually drive A.
- Either can be the current drive.
- The MS-DOS prompt shows the current drive: 'C>'.
- You can change current drives by C>**A:** or A>**C:**.
- A floppy disk must be **FORMAT**ed before being used.
- The contents of the current directory can be listed by **DIR**.
- You can move up and down the directory tree by **CD**.
- The root directory is called \.
- To copy files from one directory to another, use **COPY**.
- You can delete files completely by **ERASE**.
- You can rename files by **RENAME**.

Exercises

1 Write down a hardware specification for your installation. Enter the details in a small notebook for further reference. Possible headings:

Processor type.
Hard disk capacity.
Floppy disk size.
Display characteristics.
Graphics input device type.
Printer plotter.
Plotter.

2 Find out about the following MS-DOS commands:

DATE	**CHKDSK**
TIME	**DISKCOPY**
PROMPT	**TYPE**
MKDIR	**BACKUP**
RMDIR	**RESTORE**

Write a description of the action of each command in your notebook.

2 AutoCAD – basics

How to run AutoCAD. The layout of the drawing editor display. The AutoCAD command structure. How to learn AutoCAD effectively. Introduction to the commands **HELP**, **DRAW**, **LINE**, **UTILITIES** and **END**.

Running AutoCAD

Your AutoCAD will have been delivered on a set of disks. The programs and data stored on these disks must be transferred to your hard disk and the system then 'configured'. We have already pointed out that AutoCAD can run with a wide variety of graphics boards, plotters and graphics input devices; the system must be informed of the particular set of devices which are to be used. Most of the devices have their own operating methods and commands since there is still very little standardization in computer hardware. If the AutoCAD program contained all the instructions for dealing with all the combinations of peripherals, then it would be very much larger than it already is. This problem is solved by providing specialized drivers for each device supported by AutoCAD. These are separate from the main AutoCAD program and a set of them comes with the AutoCAD system. Full details of installation and configuration are given in the *AutoCAD Installation and Performance Guide*.

If you have installed AutoCAD yourself, you will know exactly where the AutoCAD system is stored in the directory structure. If not, then you must either ask someone or find it yourself. You will probably find it in a subdirectory called ACAD or AUTOCAD or some similarly descriptive name, the directory structure being something like that shown in Figure 1.1. After logging into this directory, AutoCAD can be run by typing **ACAD**. You will then hear some hard disk activity and a sign-on message will appear. After typing **RETURN** a couple of times, the AutoCAD main menu will appear

```
                    A U T O C A D
         Copyright (C) 1982,83,84,85,86,87,88 Autodesk, Inc.
         Release 10 (10/27/88) IBM PC
         Advanced Drafting Extensions 3
         Serial Number :    ############

         Main Menu

         0.   Exit AutoCAD
         1.   Begin a NEW drawing
         2.   Edit an EXISTING drawing
         3.   Plot a drawing
         4.   Printer Plot a drawing

         5.   Configure AutoCAD
         6.   File Utilities
         7.   Compile shape/font description file
         8.   Convert old drawing file

      Enter selection :
```

Figure 2.1   Menu

(Figure 2.1). This contains nine numbered options and selection may be made by typing the appropriate number. The actions of the options are:

0 **Exit AutoCAD**. Returns you to the operating system.

1 **Begin a NEW drawing**. Requires a drawing name in answer to a prompt. This should comply with the usual MS-DOS rules except that it should not have an extension since it is supplied with the standard extension '.DWG' automatically. On entry, a drawing can be set up in an initial environment which is determined by a prototype drawing; for example, a new drawing can be started with a standard drafting sheet already in position. If the drawing name is identical with one already stored, then a warning message will be displayed and the name changed if desired.

2 **Edit an EXISTING drawing**. Again a drawing name is required. If a drawing with that name cannot be found, then an error message is output. If all is well, then the existing drawing will be displayed in exactly the same form that it had when it was previously stored away.

3 **Plot a drawing**. This option is used if you wish to create a pen-plot of the drawing.

4 **Printer-plot a drawing**. Many printers, including ink-jet and laser types, allow you to produce a reasonably good plot of the drawing.

5 **Configure AutoCAD**. This is the option used for the process of tailoring the system to suit the equipment with which it is to be used.

6 **File utilities**. Enables all the commoner file management operations to be performed in the AutoCAD system, rather than in the operating system. A sub-menu is displayed and by selecting its options you can list drawing files or files in general, and delete, rename and copy files. This can also be done later on while you are drawing.

7 **Compile shape/font file**. This will be described later; it is not very useful for everyday drafting.

8 **Convert old drawing file**. Permits the drawings produced by old versions of AutoCAD to be made compatible with newer versions.

After you have successfully selected an option, the drawing editor screen (Figure 2.2) is displayed and you can start drawing.

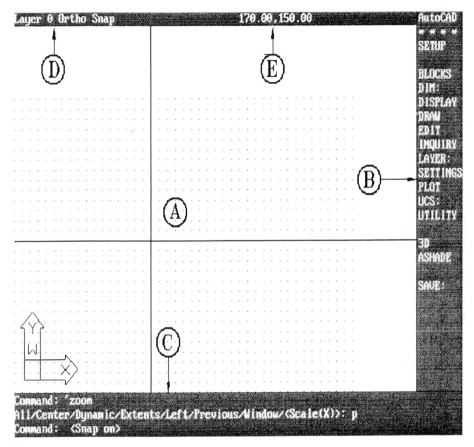

Figure 2.2 Drawing editor screen

AutoCAD commands

Figure 2.2 shows the most common layout of the screen, although it is possible to modify this through the **Configure AutoCAD** option in the main menu. The screen is partitioned into the following areas:

A Drawing space.
B Menu strip.
C Prompt area.
D Status line.
E Coordinate read-out.

A *Drawing space* is the working area for drafting. The crosshair cursor is used to move around the area and point to items of interest.

11

B The *menu strip* is used to display commands; these may be picked by moving the cursor to point to the desired command and then, by pressing a button, to select it. As the cursor moves down the vertical list of commands, feedback about its position is obtained by the current position being highlighted rather than by display of a crosshair. At first cursor control might seem awkward, but after a short while it becomes almost an unconscious procedure.

C The *prompt area* is the portion of the display set aside for system communication with the user. Typed data is echoed here, and prompts from AutoCAD are displayed including requests for information and error messages.

D The *status line* is the area set aside for showing the current condition of the drafting procedures. System settings such as **ORTHO**, which forces lines to be horizontal and vertical, are displayed.

E If you wish, you can obtain a continually updated read-out of the current cursor position. This is written in the *coordinate read-out area*.

While you are drawing, it pays to be alert to the state of all these areas and, since they are in fixed positions on the screen, they can be checked with a brief glance. Try to get into the habit of doing this regularly. It will save you a lot of trouble and improve your drafting productivity.

When the prompt 'Command:' appears in the prompt area (area C in Figure 2.2), the system is expecting a command. This wait state can be achieved at any time by typing **CTRL-C**; i.e. by holding down the key marked 'Control' and simultaneously typing 'C'. This is an escape sequence which can be used if you get stuck in the middle of a command sequence and do not know how to get out more gracefully. The fastest way to enter a command at this point is to type the one character **RETURN** which has the effect of repeating the last command. If you are using a multi-button mouse, one of the buttons will be programmed to transmit **RETURN**; often the leftmost button is used to pick items from the display and the rightmost is used for **RETURN**.

The most basic (and, possibly, the slowest) way of entering a command is to type it on the keyboard. This will usually produce further prompts; for instance:

Command:**LINE**
From point:

Another method is to pick the command from the menu strip down the right hand side of the screen (B on Figure 2.2). There are far too many commands in AutoCAD to display on the screen at one time without severely limiting the space reserved for drawing. This problem is solved by dividing the commands into groups – for example, the **DRAW** group contains twenty-two commands of which one is **LINE**. The system starts by displaying the names of these groups in the root menu (Figure 2.1). When an option is picked from the root menu, a more specialized menu appears; in certain cases, the procedure may be repeated. The commands are then organized in a tree-like structure. When the root menu option **DRAW** is picked, it is again impossible to accommodate the whole twenty-two commands in the menu area, so the system displays just the first twelve, with an option **next** at the bottom of the menu. If this is picked, the remaining ten options are displayed. So, assuming that the root menu was on display and we wished to select the command **TEXT**, we should have to use the following pick sequence: **DRAW-next-TEXT**. A list of AutoCAD commands and their associated main menu items is given in Appendix B.

There is no need to observe the grouped structure if the commands are typed; the single typed command **TEXT** would have the same effect. Notice, however, that the latter method would require five keystrokes while the cursor pick method would only need three.

Yet another way to enter commands is to use *pull-down* menus if your display supports this feature. If you move the cursor to the top of the screen (the status line) using the input device, a menu bar appears. This is a horizontal strip containing seven items which represent another grouping of the commands (Figure 2.3).

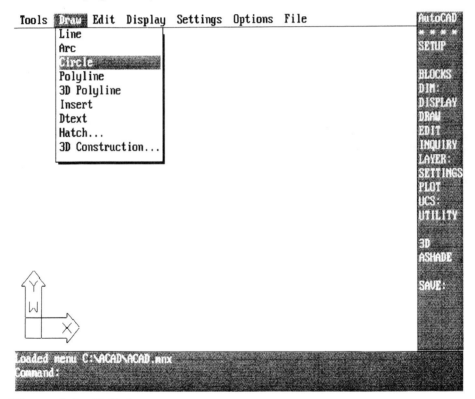

Figure 2.3 Pull-down menu

If an item on this menu bar is picked, then another menu is pulled down from which items may be picked. The range of options on the pull-down menus is smaller than the full range available on the vertical right hand menu, but all the most useful commands are catered for. Several of the options result in *dialogue boxes* being displayed (Figure 2.4 shows an example of a dialogue box).

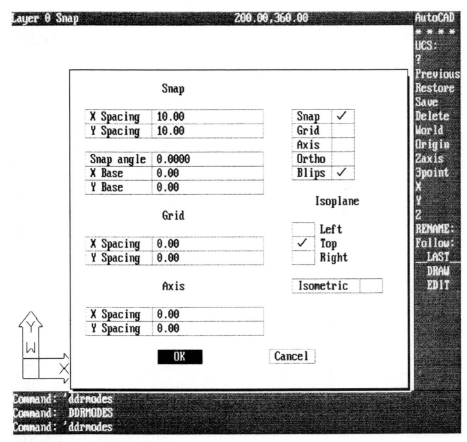

Figure 2.4 Dialogue box

Options can be selected from the dialogue box and the normal display returns when 'OK' is picked. Other options result in the display of *Icon menus*, the various options being shown pictorially – Figure 2.5 shows a typical icon menu.

If you are using a digitizing tablet, then most of the commands can be selected with just one pick of the stylus or puck on a menu card. Figure 2.6 on page 16 shows the standard tablet menu card supplied with AutoCAD. The command **LINE** will be found in position 10J on this card.

A new user is, then, faced with a bewildering set of choices. Summarizing, in order to enter the command **LINE**, you can, in response to the 'Command:' prompt:

(a) Type **RETURN**, if the last command happened to be **LINE**.
(b) Type the word **LINE** then **RETURN**.
(c) Pick the option **DRAW** from the menu area on the right of the screen, then pick **LINE** from the resulting sub-menu.
(d) Pull down the menu **DRAW**, then pick **LINE** from the resulting pull-down menu.
(e) Pick the option **LINE** from the tablet, if you have one.

When you first start using AutoCAD, it is probably best to use method (c)

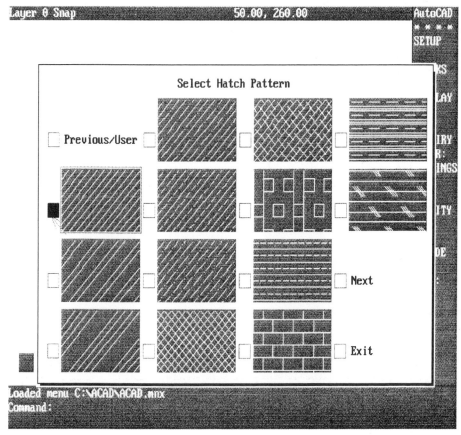

Figure 2.5 Icon menu

exclusively, picking commands from the menu strip on the right of the display. After a while, you will become accustomed to the menu structure and incorporate other methods into your mode of working. In most of the examples in this book, in the interests of standardization, we mainly assume that the commands are typed. If you are using method (c), you will have to find the route through the menu yourself. This will speed the process of learning to find your way round the system. There is no *best* way of using AutoCAD; there is a best way for you. This will vary as you become used to the system and become more proficient. Eventually, like most other skilled operators, you will settle on a combination of several methods.

How to learn AutoCAD

When you are new to AutoCAD, a very useful aid is the on-line **HELP** facility. On entry to the system, the graphics editor screen is displayed. This is the screen on which the drafting is done. There is also a text screen available and the two screens can be interchanged (or flipped) by input of commands or, more conveniently, by hitting a function key – the usual one is F1. A key acting in this way is known as a 'toggle'. A list of other toggle keys

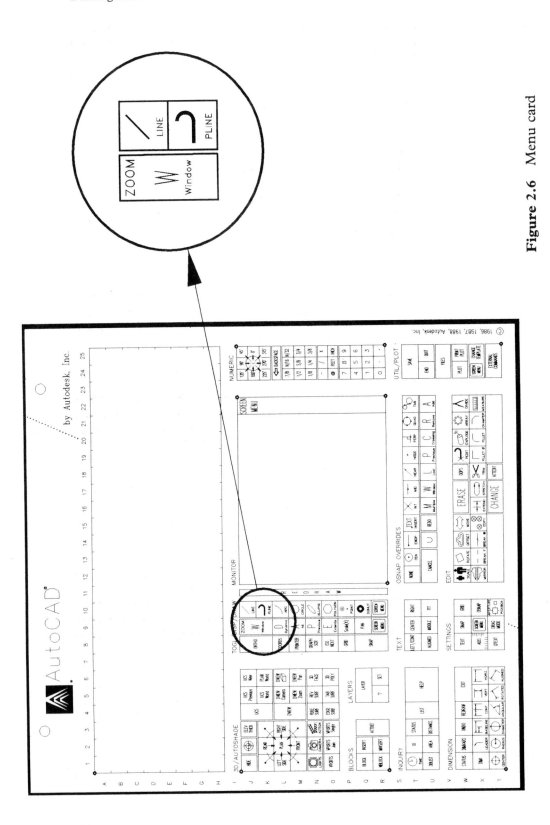

Figure 2.6 Menu card

is shown for reference in Table 2.1 and, although the use of most of them will not yet be apparent, it will improve your speed if you learn them by heart when they have been explained.

Table 2.1   Toggle keys

CTRL-B	Snap toggle	F1	Screen flip
CTRL-C	Abort command	F6	Coords toggle
CTRL-D	Coordinate display	F7	Grid toggle
CTRL-G	Display grid toggle	F8	Ortho toggle
CTRL-H	Backspace	F9	Snap toggle
CTRL-O	Ortho toggle	F10	Tablet toggle
CTRL-Q	Print echo toggle		
CTRL-T	Tablet mode toggle		
CTRL-X	Delete all characters		

The text screen is used in AutoCAD to display quite comprehensive information about the AutoCAD commands and how they are used. The command **HELP** or **?** may be used when you are uncertain about how to proceed; it results in the following prompt being issued to the user:

Command name (RETURN for list):

Entering **RETURN** causes a list of valid commands to be displayed on the text screen. Repeating the **RETURN** results in a further list. Another **RETURN** initiates a display of information about the definition of coordinates. You can exit from this command by typing **CTRL-C** as usual.

If you answer the prompt with a command name, then details of the command usage are shown on the text screen. This version of **HELP** is used at the command prompt but **HELP**, like many other commands, can be used in the middle of another command. This transparent help is obtained by typing **'HELP**. Apart from the apostrophe, the process is completely the same. **HELP** is a most useful facility when you are trying to get to grips with a new software package but in some systems the assistance obtained is rather disappointing. This is not so in AutoCAD; the information obtained is quite comprehensive.

The best way to learn AutoCAD (or any other system) is to experiment with it. The most effective way to experiment is not to flail around trying all the commands successively but to set yourself goals and find different ways of achieving them. You will find Appendix B useful. Probably the best technique is to sketch something roughly and then draw it in AutoCAD.

And now it is about time that you had a browse around the AutoCAD system. You will find it advantageous to have a small notebook in which you can write down your discoveries and difficulties. It is useful to note the AutoCAD command conventions:

(a)   Options are shown separated by a slash.
(b)   Options are usually shown in full and their legal abbreviations indicated by being displayed in upper case letters.

(c) Defaults are often supplied. These are shown enclosed by the brackets '<' and '>'.

An example is:

Command:**CHAMFER**
Polyline/Distance/<Select first line>:

Here, Polyline is an option which can be abbreviated to 'P'. The default option is <Select first line>.

Example. A quick look at AutoCAD

Brief
Firstly, to investigate the AutoCAD menu system and **HELP** facility and to get some practice in using the drawing editor. Secondly, to develop confidence in using the system in an investigatory way.

Plan of action
Enter AutoCAD and examine the menus using the cursor. Next, demonstrate the method of flipping from the graphics screen to the text screen. Examine the methods of inputting commands and quitting them prematurely. Practice the use of the **HELP** facility. Use drawing commands to put marks on the screen and use **ERASE** to remove them. Save the resulting drawing, then quit the system. Re-enter the system, call up the drawing you have just saved and then freely experiment with the system.

Command sequence
Find the directory containing the AutoCAD system; it will probably be in the sub-directory ACAD. Log into that directory and then run AutoCAD:

C>**CD ACAD**
C>**ACAD**

You will then see a welcome message appear. Type **RETURN** once or twice until the main menu (Figure 2.1) appears on the screen. Type option number 1 and then enter the drawing name (BROWSE1 will do). There will then be some activity and the drawing editor will be displayed (Figure 2.2). Use your mouse or other graphics input device to move the cursor around the screen.

It is profitable at this stage to find a comfortable working position. Move your chair close enough to the screen so that you can reach the keyboard and graphics input device without leaning forward. You can adjust the positions of the equipment to suit yourself; for example, if you are using a stylus and tablet the connector is probably long enough for you to hold the tablet on your lap if you find it comfortable. Adjust the brightness of the display so that the lines are as sharp as possible. This is more important than their being as bright as possible. A bright but fuzzy display will tire your eyes more than a dim but sharp one.

You will possibly find it difficult to control the cursor movement with

---

the graphics input device at first but don't worry; in a short time it will be as mechanical as pointing with your finger. If you are using a mouse, then it may be possible to adjust the sensitivity to your liking but it is best to leave this until you are a little more experienced with the system. You can operate the mouse with your left hand if you prefer it. Some of the slickest operators use the left hand for operating the mouse and reserve the right hand for typing.

Notice how the cursor positional coordinates shown at the end of the status line change as you move the cursor around (B on Figure 2.2). If this cursor read-out is not happening, then you can switch it on by typing **CTRL-D**. Move the cursor to the vertical menu area on the right; notice how the options are highlighted as you move up and down the menu strip.

You will find it useful to refer to Figure 2.2 which shows the drawing editor display. Move the cursor (by moving your graphics input device) to the top of the screen in a position above the drawing area. If your equipment allows it, a menu bar will appear. Move the cursor along this menu bar and notice how each of the options is highlighted in turn.

Move to the menu strip on the right and move the cursor until it is over the option **DRAW** and then hit the button on your graphics input device. If **DRAW** is not being displayed, then you have been enterprising and doing a little investigation of your own. You should pick the AutoCAD option at the extreme top of the menu strip which will result in the root menu being displayed; **DRAW** is an option on the root menu. The result of picking **DRAW** is the display of a sub-menu, one option of which is **LINE**. Pick **LINE**. Another sub-menu will be displayed and also, in the prompt area at the bottom of the screen, will appear the prompt 'First point:'.

Now change your mind. You are in the middle of a command and the system is in state of expectancy; it wants you to define the first point of a line. Return to the command prompt by typing **CTRL-C**.

Depress the function key F1. The screen will flip and the text screen will replace the graphics screen. You will see a record of your transactions with the computer so far. Flip back by pressing F1 again.

It's about time we did some drawing. If you have followed the instructions so far, the last command you entered was **LINE**. You do not need to re-input it in this case; just hit the **RETURN** key or, if you are using a multi-button mouse, hit a programmed button, probably the one on the extreme right. The command sequence is:

Command:**RETURN**
First point:

If this doesn't work, the last command was not **LINE** and you can proceed:

Command:**LINE**
First point:

You can now pick the start point of the line. The next prompt will be:

To point:

As you move the cursor around the screen, you will notice a line joining the crosshair position to the first point that you picked. This useful feature is called 'rubber-banding'. When the cursor arrives at the desired position, press the pick button again. You have now drawn the first of your many AutoCAD lines. You can carry on picking further points to complete further line segments.

When you have drawn enough lines, you can leave the command by hitting **RETURN** on the keyboard or on your mouse. Or you can type **CTRL-C** which requires two hands and so is more inconvenient.

You have used an AutoCAD command but in a primitive way. If you want to find out more about **LINE**, at the Command: prompt enter **HELP LINE**. The screen will flip from graphics to text modes and you will be into the on-line help facility. An explanation of the command and its use will be displayed. When you have read enough, return to the Command: prompt by **CTRL-C**, then flip back to graphics by the function key F1.

Now enter **LINE** again. It is not necessary to go down the command chain **AutoCAD > DRAW > LINE** every time you wish to draw a set of connected lines. At the bottom of most sub-menus are the two options **DRAW** and **EDIT**, which can be picked directly. Or you can pick the **DRAW** option from the horizontal menu bar at the top of the screen and then **LINE** from the resulting pull-down menu. Or you might consider it most convenient to type **LINE** on the keyboard. For the moment, it is better to restrict yourself to one method. Draw a few lines.

You can now save the drawing for future reference. Pick **UTILITIES** from the root menu and then **END**. The drawing will be saved and you will leave the graphics editor. After some hard disk activity, the AutoCAD main menu will be redisplayed. You can return to the operating system by selecting option 0.

If you wish to exit without saving the drawing, pick **QUIT**. Since this is rather drastic, the system will ask you for confirmation before proceeding. You can also save your drawing without leaving the system by picking **SAVE**. It is beneficial to use this command every now and then during the course of a drafting session. This will limit the damage caused by a system failure.

In the operating system you can check that your drawing has been stored by getting a list of all the drawings on file by:

DIR *.DWG

because all AutoCAD drawings have the extension '.DWG'.

Now re-enter the AutoCAD system. At the main menu, pick option 2 to edit an existing drawing and then type **BROWSE1** when you are asked for the drawing name. Your drawing will appear in exactly the same state as when you stored it. You can now investigate the commands **LINE**, **CIRCLE** and **ERASE**, getting **HELP** when you cannot guess how to use a command.

Exercises

1 Try to draw each of the five shapes shown in Figure 2.7 with a minimum number of separate **LINE** commands. There are two that you will not be able to do in one command; see if you can reason out why this is (nothing to do with AutoCAD!). In this and the next exercise, there is no need for your drawings to be dimensionally precise (unless you have done a bit of private investigation). They are intended just to provide practice in using the drawing cursor.

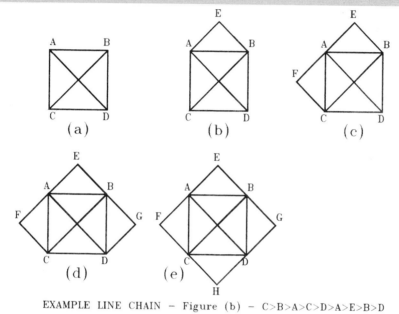

EXAMPLE LINE CHAIN – Figure (b) – C>B>A>C>D>A>E>B>D

Figure 2.7   Exercise: LINE command

2 Draw some of the shapes in Figure 2.8. Try to keep the proportions approximately correct.

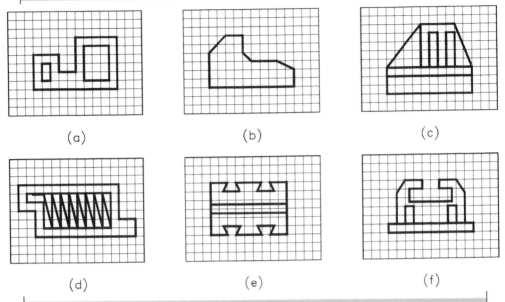

(a)   (b)   (c)

(d)   (e)   (f)

Figure 2.8   Exercise: LINE command

3 Find the following commands starting from the main screen menu:

COPY:	**ELLIPSE:**
REGEN:	**AREA:**
MIRROR:	**STYLE:**
POINT:	**BLIPS:**
HOMETEXT:	**FILES:**

The colon at the end of a command indicates that it leads to a sub-menu and stops execution of a current command. If you have time, use the **HELP** facility to find out what the commands are for. If you have difficulty, the command list in Appendix B should be helpful.

3	# Drafting – basics

A survey of some of the principles of good drawing office practice. International standards for sheet sizes, and scales. A description of first and third angle projections and the types of drawing that are commonly used in engineering.

Introduction

In this section we shall discuss some elements of drafting practice. All industrial nations have their own standards of drafting practice – in Britain, the standard is BS 308, which has been drawn on extensively in this, and subsequent, sections. Another well-known standard is the American National Standards Institute Drafting Manual which is also mentioned where appropriate. Sub-committee TC 10/SC 1 of ISO (the International Organization for Standards) is involved in the standardization of general drafting procedures; thirty leading industrial nations are involved. Although drafting standards often describe manual drafting practice, most of their recommendations may be beneficially applied to computer aided drafting also.

It is important to bear in mind that the aim of the traditional engineering drawing is to communicate information about a component in a convenient and easily-read form. This is also the paramount aim in computer aided drafting; it is not the slightest use being able to draw a complex part in a minimum number of keystrokes if the result is difficult to read. For this reason, it is best to take notice of the principles advocated in drafting standards. On the other hand, drafting standards tend to be non-prescriptive; they merely give details of devices which have been found by experts to result in a clear and unambiguous representation of a component. If there is a method of describing some feature of a component in an unorthodox but easily understandable way, it is a mistake to stick slavishly to a general standard.

Recommended sheet sizes

The metric standard for drawing sheets is the ISO 'A' Series. Their sizes are:

A0   841 mm × 1189 mm
A1   594 mm × 841 mm
A2   420 mm × 594 mm
A3   297 mm × 420 mm
A4   210 mm × 297 mm

The dimensions are worked out very carefully. The A0 sheet has an area of very nearly 1 square metre. Each sheet has sides in the ratio of $\sqrt{2}:1$, which means that if a sheet is halved along the longer side, then the result will be two sheets of the next smaller size. This halving procedure can be continued right down to the 35 mm microfilm size. The standard microfilm reduction ratios (14.8, 21, 29.7) are also in this ratio. Engineering drawings more often than not have the longer side horizontal – the 'landscape' aspect ratio.

American National Standard sheet sizes are:

E   34 × 44 inches
D   22 × 34 inches
C   17 × 22 inches
B   11 × 17 inches
A   8.5 × 11 inches

The difference between the ISO A4 and the ANSI A sheets is a complication for printers, which are often switchable from one size to another to accommodate the two sizes of stationery.

Drafting sheets

It is usual for firms to use a standard drafting sheet for engineering drawings, although in some fields, such as tool design, it is common for plain paper to be used. The majority of large engineering firms use pre-printed drafting sheets because plotting is still an expensive operation. Smaller installations often plot the drafting sheet along with the component.

Since most drawings are reproduced in some way for distribution and for record purposes, it is undesirable that the drafting should be done right up to the edge of the cut sheet. It is recommended that a frame should be printed inside the standard sheet so that there is a border that can be used for registration purposes. BS 308 recommends a border at least 15 mm wide all round the drawing area. The ANSI recommendation is for a border of 0.25 inches. Larger drawing sheets often have fold marks (there is even a standard for folding drawings!) and grid references for identifying items on a drawing in documentation.

The engineering drawing is the major record of information about a product and it is usual for drawings to carry a lot of non-graphical data. The firm's name is prominently displayed, there are boxes for the drawing number and tables for issue and amendment information. Much of this kind of information is localized in a detailed title block which contains basic information such as:

The drawing title
The original scale
Date drawn
Drafter's signature
Date checked.
Checker's initials
Unit of measurement
Type of projection (1st or 3rd)
Copyright note

In addition to a definition of the geometric form of the component, its drawing often contains details of the manufacturing process, specifications of materials, finishes and details of gauging methods and so on. BS 308 gives a list (not exhaustive) of 32 items of information that can be shown on a drawing. It is a wonder that there is any room for drawing the component at all. Fortunately, computer aided drafting does not require all the information held on a drawing to be displayed at once.

Throughout this book, we shall be using a simple plotted drafting sheet (Figure 3.1), which will be constructed in a subsequent chapter.

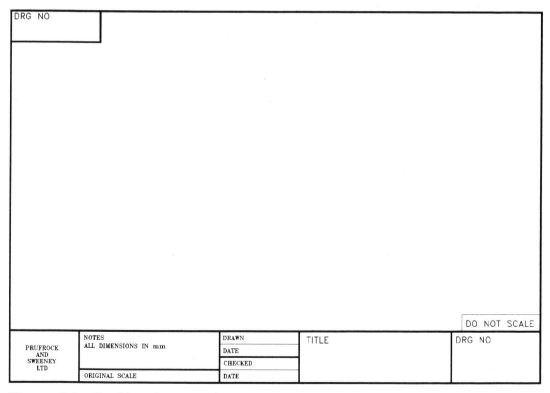

Figure 3.1 Drafting sheet

Types of drawing

There are various kinds of drawing used in engineering and the selection used in a particular drawing office depends on the field of application and local practice and standards. It is advisable that a separate drawing should be prepared for each manufactured component; the drawing can consist of more than one sheet and is called a 'single part drawing'.

A mechanical device usually comprises several components and these may be shown fitted together on an assembly drawing. An assembly drawing which shows the whole of a device is called a 'general assembly drawing' (or 'GA'). Normally, a GA has an associated parts list, which may be on a separate sheet.

If a company provides a range of products differing only in size, the whole range may be conveniently shown on one drawing. This is a 'collective single part drawing'. In some areas, such as heavy engineering and jig and tool design, it is the custom to detail several components on one large sheet. Such drawings are called 'combined drawings'. It is also common to detail fabricated structures on drawings of the completed form rather than to use separate component drawings.

Scales

It is good practice to draw all components accurately, but it is often inconvenient or impracticable to draw them full size. On drawings, scales are shown as ratios; for instance, a scale of 2:1 means that a component has been drawn at double its actual size. Similarly, a scale of 1:2 means that it has been drawn half size.

In the metric system, scales used on engineering drawings are based on the numbers 2, 5 and 10. The scales suggested in BS 308 are:

1000:1	50:1	2:1	1:10	1:200
500:1	20:1	1:1	1:20	1:500
200:1	10:1	1:2	1:50	1:1000
100:1	5:1	1:5	1:100	

In the imperial system, scales are based on the numbers 2, 3 and 4. For drawings reduced in size, common scales are:

1:1	1:8	1:24	1:96
1:2	1:12	1:32	1:192
1:4	1:16	1:48	

It is important, in the interests of clarity, to pick the correct size of drafting sheet and scale for the drawing of a particular component. A small drafting sheet for a complicated component will result in a drawing with congested detail, which is difficult to read. A large sheet for a simple component will be unwieldy and take up a disproportionate amount of storage space. The selection of the correct size of drafting sheet and scale is largely a matter of experience and depends on the balance between sheet size and density of information on the drawing. In computer aided drafting, such previous planning is not absolutely necessary since drawings can be easily re-scaled. However, this does waste time and it is advisable before you start drafting to spend a little while in planning the drawing.

Projections

It is widely agreed that the ability to visualize objects in three dimensions is an essential talent for designers. It is important that there should be a standard method of communicating geometrical information to other interested parties in an engineering environment and by far the most widely used method is still the traditional engineering drawing. This was probably invented by Gaspard Monge (1746–1818) and it is still serving engineers well. Formally, it is called 'parallel orthographic multiview' projection.

In order to represent a three-dimensional object on a flat piece of paper or graphics display, we need to 'project' it. We can imagine that we are looking at the object through a transparent screen (Figure 3.2). In the case shown in Figure 3.2, lines of sight are drawn from the eye (or 'station point') to points of interest on the object and the points at which the lines of sight intersect the projection plane define the projected image. This is a perspective projection.

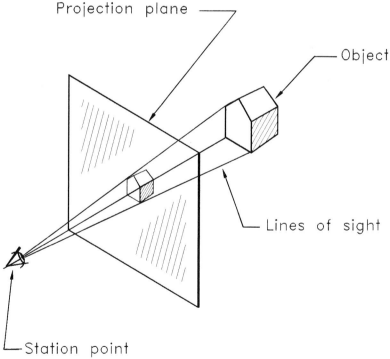

Figure 3.2   Perspective projection

If the eye is a great distance from the projection plane, then the lines of sight will be approximately parallel. They can be imagined to be *exactly* parallel and this is then a parallel projection. If the lines of sight are at right angles to the projection plane, then the projection is orthographic. We can

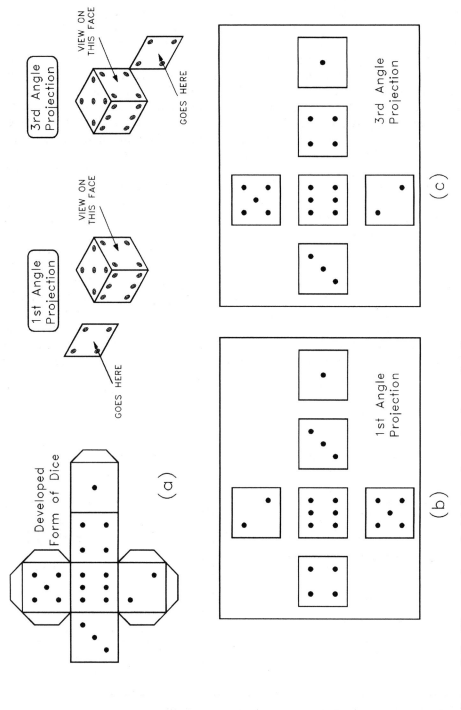

Figure 3.3 First angle and third angle projections of a dice

rotate the object to show as many views as are necessary to describe its shape. We have now arrived at the conventional engineering drawing – the parallel orthographic multiview projection.

There are two widely used ways of putting the views on the drawing to show their interrelationship: first angle and third angle projection. Most elementary textbooks on technical drafting explain the derivation of these terms; it does not concern us here. First angle projection was originally the general standard; it was replaced by third angle projection (which is more intuitively easy to interpret) in the United States about a hundred years ago and is now widely used worldwide. However, in Britain, the use of first angle projection is still prevalent and it is useful for engineers to be accustomed to both. Invariably, one or the other is declared as standard in a drawing office.

First and third angle projections differ only in the placement of the views relative to each other. Figures 3.3b and 3.3c are both correctly projected drawings of the dice shown in Figure 3.3a. Notice that the views in third angle projection are placed so that they match the developed form, each view being what would be seen looking on the near side of adjacent views. In contrast, each view in first angle projection is what would be seen looking on the further side of adjacent views.

The majority of engineering components can be defined with fewer views than the six shown in Figures 3.3b and 3.3c and just enough views should be shown to communicate the form of the component clearly. Figure 3.4 is a simple example. In this drawing, some of the hidden detail is shown in dashed lines, which is a universal convention. It is usual to select one view, usually the one which shows most detail or is most characteristic of the component, and call it the 'plan' view. Other views are called 'front and side elevations'. The conventional layouts for first and third angle projections are shown in Figure 3.4.

The conventional layout is:

First angle: The front elevation is above the plan view.
           The side elevation is next to the front one.

Third angle: The front elevation is below the plan view.
           The side elevation is next to the front one.

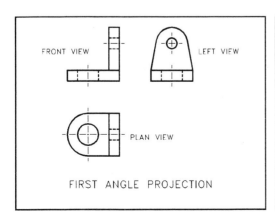
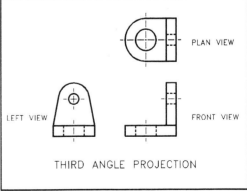

Figure 3.4 Projections of a simple component

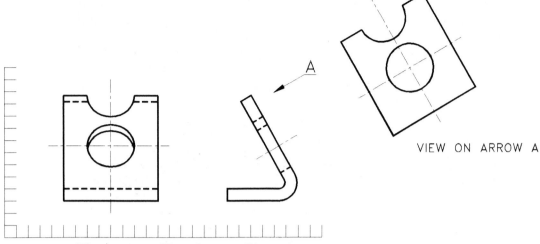

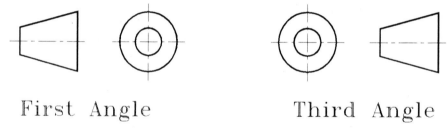

VIEW ON ARROW A

Figure 3.5 Use of an auxiliary view

If the form of a component does not lend itself easily to the sort of layout shown in Figure 3.4, then it is permissible to use auxiliary views (Figure 3.5). It is good practice to show the direction of viewing by an arrow even if the auxiliary view is in correct first or third angle position.

It is standard practice to point out the type of projection being used by a symbol – Figure 3.6 shows the form recommended by BS 308.

First Angle   Third Angle

Figure 3.6 Projection symbols

Again, you will find it beneficial to spend a little time in planning your drawing even when you are using a computer aided drafting system.

Exercises

1 Sketch, on paper, first and third angle projected drawings of some of the bodies shown in Figure 3.7. Keep the sketches. You will be drawing them in AutoCAD later.

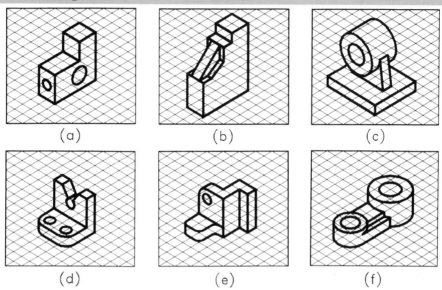

(a)   (b)   (c)

(d)   (e)   (f)

Figure 3.7   Exercise: Projections

2 Sketch the view missing from each of Figures 3.8 and 3.9.

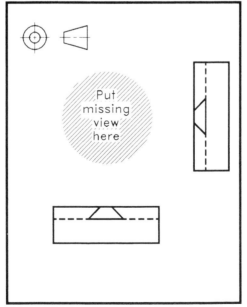

Figure 3.8   Exercise: Projections

Figure 3.9 Exercise: Projections

3   Sketch a three-dimensional view of the bodies in Figures 3.4 and
    3.5, trying to convey as much geometrical information as is con-
    tained in the projected drawings.

<table>
<tr>
<td>

4

</td>
<td>

Displays and coordinates

</td>
</tr>
</table>

A description of the ways in which the graphics display can be manipulated for maximum working convenience and productivity. The main commands covered are **USICON, UCS, REDRAW, REGEN, UNITS, LIMITS, ZOOM, PAN** and **VIEWPORT**.

Introduction

In AutoCAD, drawing is done in a rectangular area that, for all practical purposes, may be considered to be infinite. Actually, AutoCAD is a three-dimensional system but, since we are only concerned with two-dimensional drafting, we shall not bother with one of the dimensions. Points in this 'infinite' rectangular area may be referred to by quoting a pair of numbers, the X–Y coordinates. This coordinate system is known as the 'world coordinate system' or 'WCS'. There is also a second set of coordinates known as the 'user coordinate system' or 'UCS' which can be shifted around the WCS at the user's convenience. The UCS can coincide with the WCS but is often placed at a different location and orientation during the course of a drawing by the command **UCS**. This is much the same procedure as is carried out in manual drafting when the drawing is initially laid out with separate datums for each view. The position of the UCS origin is shown by an icon (which is shown at the bottom left hand corner of Figure 2.2) The display of the icon can be enabled and disabled by use of the command **UCSICON**.

It is a convenience, sometimes, to restrict the drawing to a defined part of the infinite drawing plane. Often, we wish to draw inside the bounds of a standard drawing sheet with the drawing being plotted to a standard scale. The drawing can be bounded by setting limits on the rectangular area which can be used for drawing; the system can then refuse any attempt made to draw outside the bounds set. The command **LIMITS** is used to set the legal area relative to the WCS and to enable or disable limits checking.

It is less usual to work on the whole drawing than to use magnified sections of it. We can **ZOOM** into or out of the drawing and the currently displayed **window** can be moved around the drawing using the command **PAN**. For convenience in zooming, the rectangle bounding all the drawn objects is called the *extents* of the drawing; the larger of the extents and the limits is called *all*.

AutoCAD allows users to partition the screen into up to four *viewports*. Each of these is capable of displaying a different view of the drawing independently. It is sometimes useful in two-dimensional drafting to partition the screen into two viewports and to work on one viewport while displaying the whole component, or a view of a component, on the other. Only one viewport – the current viewport – can be worked on at a time.

Coordinates

Points are specified in the current UCS. Coordinates are:

- Absolute: Coordinates are entered as a pair of decimal numbers separated by a comma. These are relative to the UCS origin.
- Relative: Coordinates may be entered relative to the previous point defined. These are a pair of decimal numbers separated by a comma and prefixed by the character '@'.
- Polar coordinates: Another way of specifying a point relative to the previously defined point is to use polar coordinates. A polar coordinate is a pair of numbers separated by the character '<' and prefixed by the character '@'. The first number of the pair is the polar radius, the second number is the polar angle.

Example. **Coordinates**

Brief
To investigate the different coordinate modes.

Plan of action
A rectangle 60 × 30 is to be drawn in various ways. The bottom left corner is at the point (100, 100).

Command sequence

Version (a): Absolute	Version (b): Relative
Command:**LINE**	Command:**LINE**
First point:**100,100**	First point:**100,100**
Next point:**160,100**	Next point:**@60,0**
Next point:**160,130**	Next point:**@0,30**
Next point:**100,130**	Next point:**@−60,0**
Next point:**100,100**	Next point:**@0,−30**
Next point:**RETURN**	Next point:**RETURN**

Version (c): Polar   Version (d): Mixed
Command:**LINE**   Command:**LINE**
First point:**100,100**   First point:**100,100**
Next point:**60<0**   Next point:**@60,0**
Next point:**30<90**   Next point:**–30<270**
Next point:**60<180**   Next point:**100,130**
Next point:**30<–90**   Next point:**C**
Next point:**RETURN**   Next point:**RETURN**

Note the **C** which closes the figure in (d).

Redraw and regenerate

When entities are drawn, the points of definition are shown on the drawing by small temporary marks called 'blips'. The generation of blips can be controlled by using the command **BLIPMODE** which permits their drawing to be switched on or off, but it is useful to have them displayed for checking purposes. **BLIPMODE** is an example of a system variable of which Auto-CAD has ninety. The values of many system variables can be adjusted using the command **SETVAR**. A list of system variables may be found in Appendix B. Often, erasing entities leaves gaps in other entities. Blips and gaps in entities result in the displayed drawing becoming untidy and, eventually, it is necessary to clear up the drawing. This is done by using the command **REDRAW** which produces a clean drawing. **REDRAW** can be used during the course of other commands. Since a redraw does not involve any calculation, it is comparatively quick. **REDRAW** only operates on the current viewport; all viewports can be cleared by **REDRAWALL**.

Rather a slower process is *regeneration* which may occur when the displayed image is changed. A display screen is composed of a rectangular array of pixels – 640 × 350, for instance. In order to draw the lines which make up an object, the appropriate pixels must be turned on. Displays have their own addressing system for referring to pixels and so the drawing coordinates must be converted to pixel addresses before the object can be drawn. This process involves a lot of calculation involving numbers with decimal parts and so is comparatively slow. If the displayed image is changed (for a zoom, for instance), the pixel addresses must be re-calculated. This process is called 'regeneration' and it can take a long time for a complex drawing to be regenerated. While regeneration is taking place, AutoCAD attempts to pacify the impatient user by announcing 'Regenerating the drawing . . .' but a long regeneration not only means that drawing takes longer but also is annoying and disturbs the flow of work.

Regeneration may be performed automatically each time an action which changes the drawing sufficiently takes place. However, it is sometimes possible to defer it until several such actions have occurred. This is done by using the command **REGENAUTO** to enable or disable automatic regeneration. If automatic regeneration is switched off, it is under the control of the user to some extent and may be enabled and disabled by using **REGEN**. We would, however, recommend that to start with you should work with automatic regeneration switched on.

In order to save regeneration time, AutoCAD can have an imaginary or 'virtual' screen which is much larger than the real screen. A section of the drawing is regenerated to this virtual screen, so if the display is zoomed or panned, the new display may only involve simple arithmetic on whole numbers which is much faster than arithmetic on numbers with decimal parts. This facility can be controlled by the command **VIEWRES** which permits zoom time to be traded off against virtual regeneration time. We would recommend you not to use fast zooms but to permit AutoCAD to use a virtual screen.

Commands associated with the display

When you enter the AutoCAD drawing editor, limits, blipmodes and other conditions are set by a 'prototype' drawing. Prototype drawings will be discussed in more detail later; if one has not been defined, the default ACAD.DWG is assumed. The drawing characteristics set by this default may not be those required – for instance, it is very likely that it will be necessary to set new limits. A fundamental setting is the format of numbers, which may be controlled by using the command **UNITS**. The command sequence is:

Command:**UNITS**
Systems of units: (Examples)
1 Scientific   1.55E+01
2 Decimal   15.50
3 Engineering   1'-3.50"
4 Architectural   1'-3 1/2"
5 Fractional   15 1/2
Enter choice, 1 to 5 <default value>:

We shall be using the metric system and so will choose option 2. If this is chosen, the sequence continues:

Number of digits to right of decimal point (0 to 8)<default>:

The number input will depend on the type of engineering that you are engaged in; we shall use two decimal places. The command continues with the specification of angles in much the same way.

Probably the next setting to be made will be that of the drawing limits. The command **LIMITS** acts as follows:

Command:**LIMITS**
ON/OFF/<Lower left corner> <current value>:

ON and OFF control whether the system permits objects to be drawn outside limits. The world coordinates of the lower left hand corner of the limits rectangle can be set by input of a coordinate in the normal way; if you are satisfied with the current values, then **RETURN** will retain them. You will then be asked for the coordinates of the upper right corner.

The position of the UCS origin is controlled by the command **UCS**. The command returns a prompt with many options:

Origin/ZAxis/3point/Entity/View/X/Y/Z/Prev/Restore/Save/Del/?/
<World>:

Some of these options are specifically to do with three-dimensional work, so we shall not be concerned with them. We can abbreviate all these options by their first letters and the relevant cases are:

O   Defines the new origin relative to the coordinates of the current UCS.

Z   Rotates the current UCS around an axis perpendicular to the screen. The system then prompts:

    Rotation angle about Z axis <0.0>:

You can now specify an angle by typing it or by picking two points on a line at the required angle. This is useful when part of the dimension system of a drawing is at an angle (Figure 5.1 on page 45 illustrates a typical case).

W   Makes the UCS coincide with the WCS.

P   Returns to the previous UCS. This is a very useful option since Auto-CAD remembers the ten previous settings and this enables the drafter to skip from one view of a drawing to another which is the usual way of drafting.

If you are patient enough to plan your drawings ahead, then you can set up separate UCS's for each view of the drawing. These can be stored by name and switched by just quoting their names. The three options **S(ave)**, **D(elete)** and **R(estore)** are used to manipulate the named UCS's. Before drawing, we might set up three UCS's, possibly named: 'PELEV', 'LELEV' and 'RELEV' to act as datums on the Plan, Left and Right Elevations. Input of '?' lists all saved UCS's.

The UCS icon is redrawn (if enabled by **UCSICON**) to show the new position and/or orientation of axes. On selection of **UCSICON**, a list of options is displayed:

    ON/OFF/All/Noorigin/ORigin<current ON/OFF state>:

ON and **OFF** should be self-explanatory; the other options govern how the icon is displayed. **Noorigin** places the icon at the bottom left hand corner of the viewport; **ORigin** attempts to place it at the UCS origin, but if it is off-screen, then it is placed at the bottom left hand corner.

Notice that the abbreviation for **ORigin** cannot be **O**, since this would be ambiguous; in order to stop any confusion with **OFF** and **ON**, the abbreviation is **OR**. Another useful point is that, if the icon is situated at the origin of the UCS, it contains a '+'; if it coincides with the WCS origin, a 'W' appears.

A dialog box can be used to set your UCS conveniently if your display will allow it.

Zoom

Probably the most commonly used operation in computer aided drafting is zooming. If you wish to achieve a high degree of productivity, it is important that you should become as adept as possible in using the AutoCAD **ZOOM** command which may be found in the main menu item **DRAW**. Displaying magnified sections of the drawing may be done for several reasons. Because of the comparatively coarse resolution of even a high quality screen, it is usually desirable to draw detail not on the whole drawing but on magnified sections of it. Editing congested areas of the drawing is easier if the clusters of entities are given more separation by zooming. AutoCAD gives a comprehensive battery of zoom options which may be obtained by the command:

Command:**ZOOM**
All/Centre/Dynamic/Extents/Left/Previous/Window/ < Scale(X) >:

The default option is, as may be deduced from the command prompt above, Scale(X) which expects a numeric scale factor.

The display is scaled by the factor input with the centre of the screen remaining in position. The scale factor can be greater than one, in which case objects in the drawing will be magnified, or less than one, in which case they will be diminished in size. The scale factor acts on the whole drawing. If, however, the input factor is followed by the letter 'X', the scaling will be done on the displayed view of the drawing.

The most useful (and used) options are:

- Window (W) expects and prompts for a rectangular box, enclosing the part of the drawing to be zoomed, to be specified. If this part is wholly on the display, then the box is most conveniently specified by picking its two diagonally opposite corners with the pointing device. Unlike some other drafting systems, AutoCAD retains the shape of the display on a zoom and if the zoom window is not geometrically similar to the drawing area, the window is adjusted horizontally or vertically to fill the screen. The centre of the window becomes the centre of the display. On selection of **window**, a small box is displayed at the junction of the crosshairs and the window box is displayed dynamically as it is expanded and contracted.
- All (A) zooms the display to either the drawing extents or to the limits, whichever displays the larger area.
- Previous (P) restores the previous displayed view. This is a particularly useful option since AutoCAD remembers the previous ten display conditions.

You can get by reasonably well with these three options; others are:

- Extents (E) zooms to the extents of the drawing.
- Centre (C) zooms by a specified magnification factor about a defined centre point.
- Left (L) acts like centre except that the bottom left hand corner is displayed.
- Dynamic (D) is the most powerful and the most complicated. When dynamic zoom is invoked, the display changes and the following are displayed on the screen:
    - (a) the drawing extents,
    - (b) the drawing regeneration area,
    - (c) the current view.

    On a colour system, each of these is surrounded by a distinctively coloured box. A view box can be moved around this display, then anchored positionally, then enlarged or shrunk to enclose the view to be zoomed. If the view selected lies inside the virtual regenerated area then

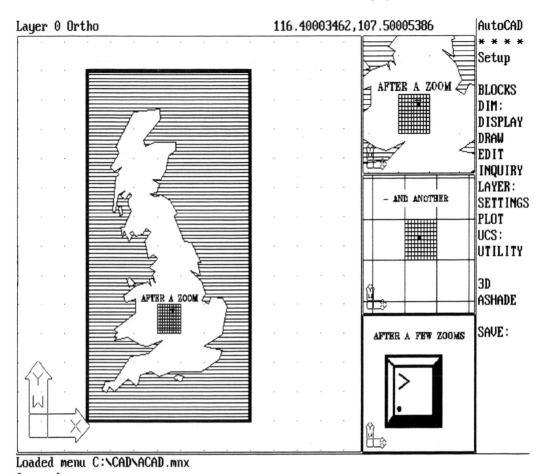

Figure 4.1 The zoom facility

no regeneration is necessary, the zoom merely needing a fast redraw.

Dynamic zoom is useful for two reasons. If a zoom of a section of drawing lies wholly or partially off the screen, then it can be done by zooming to the limits, then zooming on a window when the whole drawing is displayed. Using dynamic zoom reduces this to just one command. Also, if the window selected is even one pixel outside the virtual regeneration area, then the drawing must be regenerated. Dynamic zoom displays the virtual regeneration area. The zoom can be chosen, if possible, inside this area which results in no regeneration being needed. This option is ingenious and very useful, but it is probably best to leave it until you have developed facility with the first three recommended options described.

Figure 4.1 illustrates the power of the AutoCAD zoom facility. The drawing of Great Britain is repeatedly zoomed until eventually the display shows the decimal point on a key of a microcomputer in Birmingham Polytechnic in the West Midlands. You can work out the magnification factor yourself.

Pan

The display window can be moved around the drawing by using the **PAN** command. The command sequence is:

Command:**PAN**
Displacement:**Pick a point on the display**
Second point:**Pick the point to which the first point is to be moved**

If **RETURN** is entered instead of a second point, the first coordinate is assumed to be a relative movement. It is most convenient to pick the points with the pointing device. **PAN** can result in regeneration, so it is best to make displacement as small as possible.

View

The display in a current viewport can be named, stored and retrieved using the **VIEW** command:

Command:**VIEW**
?/Delete/Restore/Save/Window:**Pick option**
View name:**Invent name up to 31 characters long**

? lists the currently defined views.
Save stores the view in the drawing file.
Restore places the named view in the current viewport.
Window permits view definition with a window.
Delete erases a named view.

The main use of views in drafting is in plotting.

ZOOM, **PAN** and **VIEW** can be used transparently, that is, in the middle of another command. For transparent use, the command is prefixed by an apostrophe.

Viewports

AutoCAD provides a multiple viewport facility; the drafting area can be partitioned into one, two, three or four viewports. An example in which the screen has been divided into two viewports is shown in Figure 4.2. Each viewport can display a different window. In two-dimensional drafting, the screen is divided into two, and one partition is used to display the whole drawing, the other displaying a magnified view which is more conveniently worked on than would be the whole view. Any change in the magnified drawing results in the change being recorded in the whole drawing viewport. Multiple viewports are invaluable when you are working in three dimensions but they are not nearly so useful when you are drafting. One reason for this is that the aspect ratio of the display screen does not lend itself to drawing on a split screen. Also, the whole drawing can be easily examined using dynamic zoom.

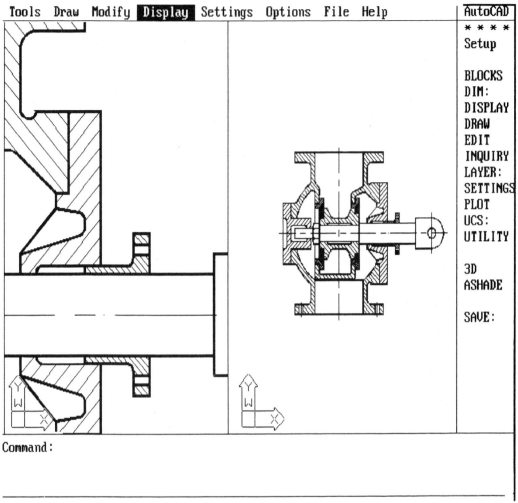

Figure 4.2 Viewports

The screen can be partitioned into viewports by the following command sequence:

Command:**VIEWPORTS**
Save/Restore/Delete/Join/Single/?/2/3/4:

- S(ave) permits the naming of a viewport configuration.
  The name can be up to 31 characters long.

- R(estore) brings back a previously defined and saved
  viewport.

- D(elete) deletes a previously named and stored part.

- J(oin) merges two viewports into one. The views must be adjacent and
  together form a rectangle.

- SI(ngle) restores the display to a single viewport.

- 2, 3, 4, divide the screen into the stated number of viewports. For two viewports, the partitioning can be in a horizontal or vertical direction. For four viewports, the screen is divided into a 2 × 2 pattern of equal-sized viewports. For three viewports, the division can be in one of a number of ways.

Viewports act somewhat like layers in that only one, the current viewport, can be worked in at any given time. The crosshair shows only inside the current viewport, outside its bounds the cursor being replaced with an arrow. The current viewport is changed by picking a point inside the new viewport.

Exercises

1   Draw, to accurate scale, some of the forms in Figure 2.8 on page 21. Take the side of a square in the grid as 10 mm.

2   Create a third angle projected drawing of the form shown in Figure 3.7b. You should have prepared a sketched drawing already. Assume that the isometric grid has a pitch of 10 mm.

5 Drawing aids – snaps and grids

A discussion of the AutoCAD facilities for snapping to existing entities and the use of snap grids. Commands covered include **SNAP**, **GRID**, **AXIS**, **ORTHO** and **APERTURE**.

Snap grids

Very often, parts of a drawing are sized in multiples of some whole number, say 5 mm. AutoCAD, like other computer aided drafting systems, provides a facility for drawing such parts very quickly indeed. It is possible to set up a grid of points at some fixed pitch and to draw by locking the cursor into points on the grid. The drawing is done in a 'join the dots' manner which is a most convenient and rapid way of working. The grid is called a *snap grid* and we say that the cursor 'snaps' to points on the grid. Most of the illustrations in this book were drawn on a snap grid of pitch 5 drawing units. Using a snap grid is also a most effective way of drawing when one is not particularly interested in dimensional precision – the AutoCAD equivalent of 'sketching on the back of an envelope'.

The command for setting up a snap grid is **SNAP**; the command sequence is;

Command:**SNAP**
Snap spacing or ON/OFF/Aspect/Rotate/Style < default pitch >:

The snap spacing is the pitch of the snap points on the grid. The pitch does not have to be the same in both X and Y directions; selection of the option **Aspect** permits a different pitch to be entered in each direction.

The **Rotate** option allows the grid to be rotated by some input angle about a base point. In this case, the command sequence is:

Command:**SNAP**
Snap spacing or ON/OFF/Aspect/Rotate/Style < 5 >:**Rotate**
Base point < 0,0 >:**Pick base point**
Rotation angle < 0 >:**Input angle**

The snap grid is aligned to the basepoint and rotated about it. It is occasionally useful to align the snap grid but preserve its original orientation. In this case, the angle of rotation prompt should be answered by **RETURN**.

The **Style** option allows a choice to be made between an isometric grid and the standard rectangular grid. The isometric grid is an aid in the drawing of isometric views and will be discussed later; for the moment we shall restrict discussion to the standard rectangular grid.

When the spacing (or snap resolution) and rotation angle have been set, snap mode can be enabled by using the **ON** or **OFF** option. It is also possible to turn snap on and off by using the keyboard toggle **CTRL-B**. When the snap grid is enabled, the word 'Snap' appears in the status line but there is no grid visible. The only visible effect (besides the entry on the status line) is that the cursor moves in a jerky fashion as it snaps to the points of the grid in its movement across the screen. A grid can be displayed using the command **GRID** and if the pitch of the points on this grid is made the same as those on the snap grid, then the action can be seen in a clearer way. The command sequence is:

Command:**GRID**
Grid spacing(X) or ON/OFF/Snap/Aspect < current spacing > :

This option line is not unlike that of **SNAP** and works broadly in the same way. **Grid spacing** and **Aspect** are like their equivalents in **SNAP** except that a grid spacing of zero is assumed to mean the current snap setting. If it is required that the grid should be displayed at a spacing that is a fixed multiple of the snap spacing, then the multiple should be entered followed by the letter 'X'. The drawings in Figure 2.8 were drawn on a snap grid of 5 mm with a displayed grid of 10 mm. The setting for grid spacing was entered as '2X'. If the grid spacing is to be the same as the snap point spacing, then the **SNAP** option can be selected, which has the same effect as setting the grid spacing to 0 but is probably more easily remembered.

ON and **OFF** behave differently from the same options in **SNAP**. In the command **GRID**, their action is just to display or turn off the matrix of grid points. The grid points are not entities and do not appear on plots; they exist just to aid drawing. The grid can be toggled on and off by using **CTRL-G**. If the pitch of the grid has been set too finely to be displayed on the screen, then a message will appear in the prompt area announcing 'Grid too dense'. The grid will not be displayed.

Example. **To draw a shape using a snap grid**

Brief
Draw the part shown in Figure 5.1.

Plan of action
On examination it is noticed that the bulk of the dimensions on this part are multiples of 10 mm. A snap grid of pitch 10 mm is selected and snap is turned on. The grid is displayed. Where the dimensions do not lie on the snap grid, dimensions are typed.

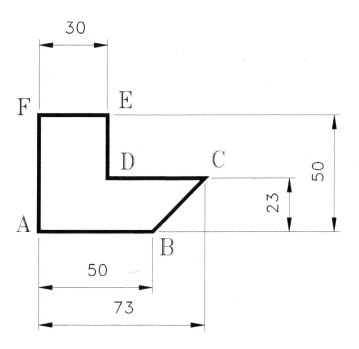

Figure 5.1   Using a snap grid

Command sequence
Set up the snap grid.

>Command:**SNAP**
>Snap spacing or ON/OFF/Aspect/Rotate/Style <5>:10
>Command:**RETURN**
>Snap spacing or ON/OFF/Aspect/Rotate/Style <10>:**ON**
>Command:**GRID**
>Grid spacing (X) or ON/OFF/Snap/Aspect <5>:**SNAP**
>Command:**CTRL-B**

The grid is turned on. 'Snap' is displayed on the status line. Now do the drawing.

>Command:**LINE**
>From point:**Pick point A on snap grid**
>To point:**Pick point B on snap grid**
>To point:**@23,23**
>To point:**Pick point D on snap grid**
>To point:**Pick point E on snap grid**
>To point:**Pick point F on snap grid**
>To point:**C**
>Command:

This simple example should illustrate how quickly drawing can be done using a snap grid. Use one at every opportunity.

Example. Rotating a snap grid

Brief
Draw the form shown in Figure 5.2.

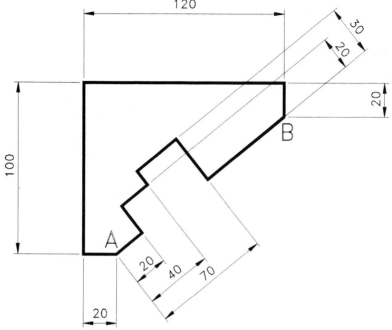

Figure 5.2   Rotating a snap grid

Plan of action
A snap grid of 10 units is set up and snap turned on. The part of the profile composed of horizontal and vertical lines is drawn by snapping to points on the grid. The snap grid is rotated so that it aligns with the rest of the profile and the form completed by snapping to the rotated grid.

Command sequence
Set up and turn on the 10 units snap grid as in the preceding example.
   Draw the form from A to B clockwise using **LINE** and snapping to points on the grid.
   Now rotate the grid:

Command:**SNAP**
Snap spacing or ON/OFF/Aspect/Rotate/Style <10>:**R**
Base point <0.00,0.00>:**Pick point A**
Rotation angle <0.00>:**Pick point B**

Complete the drawing by using the command **LINE** and snapping to points on the rotated grid.

This is the most straightforward way of drawing forms of this kind. Another, more general, way is to set up a user coordinate system with origin at point **A** and rotated so that the X-axis aligns with the line **A–B**. Coordinates can then be entered directly.

Other drafting aids: axis and ortho

If you find that a grid of small pitch is distracting, you can, of course, turn it off. But you may prefer to use another way to help you to use snap grids – the **AXIS** command. This sets up a 'ruler' of tick marks at the bottom and right edges of the drawing area. The command sequence is:

Command:**AXIS**
Tick spacing (X) or ON/OFF/Snap/Aspect < Current setting > :

This works in a similar fashion to **GRID** except that instead of a matrix of dots, tick axes are set up. Again if the setting is too fine, then the message 'Axis ticks too close to display' appears and the command is terminated.

The command **ORTHO** is also useful. It constrains all lines on a drawing to be at either 0 degrees or 90 degrees. The command sequence is:

Command:**ORTHO**
ON/OFF:**Pick ON or OFF**
Command:

There is no need to input either ON or OFF since the **ENTER** acts as a toggle. **ORTHO** can also be switched on and off by the keyboard toggle **CTRL-O**. Make sure that **ORTHO** is turned off when you have finished using it, otherwise you will get some unexpected effects when using drawing commands and osnaps which will be discussed next.

Object snap

A feature in which AutoCAD scores over many other computer-aided drafting systems is its comprehensive set of object snaps. The command **OSNAP** provides a facility for snapping to key points on existing entities. For example, if we wish to draw a line from a point tangential to a previously drawn circle, we could pick the point, select the object snap **TAN** and then pick the circle's circumference near the point of tangency. The line will be drawn automatically from the first point to the point of tangency. A possible command sequence is:

Command:**LINE**
From point:**Pick the point**
To point:**TAN**
Tangent to:**Pick circle near to tangent point**

If this facility were not available, then we would have to find the point of tangency by using a geometrical construction, which is not difficult but would severely impair drafting speed. Note that is necessary to help the system a little by giving it a hint about which of the two possible tangents is required. This is quite common in drafting systems and is an example of the cooperation between human and machine which makes for an effective system. If we want to draw a line tangential to two circles, then there are four possible options and again the system would need some help.

Using **OSNAP** considerably speeds up drafting time and it is well worth-while to acquaint yourself thoroughly with all the options, which are:

Nearest	Snaps to the point on an entity *visually* closest to the crosshairs.
Endpoint	Snaps to the closest endpoint of line or arc.
Midpoint	Snaps to the midpoint of line or arc.
Centre	Snaps to the centre of line or arc.
Node	Snaps to a point.
Quadrant	Snaps to the closest quadrant point of an arc or circle. The quadrant points are at 0, 90, 180 and 270 degrees on the arc or circle.
Intersection	Snaps to the intersection point of any two of the entities line, arc and circle.
Insert	Snaps to the closest insertion point – this will be discussed in a later section.
Perpendicular	Snaps to the point on a line, circle or arc that makes a perpendicular to that entity from the last point.
Tangent	Snaps to that point on a circle or arc which, when joined to the last point, makes a line tangent to the circle or arc.
Quick	Snaps to the first entity of the type specified that is found in the drawing file. Normally, the closest to the crosshair is found, which may take an appreciable time.
None	Turns off **OSNAP**.

The object snap menu may be displayed at any time by pointing at the line '* * * *' that is found at the top of the menu area at the right of the screen. The menu can also be obtained from the Tools pull-down menu. Object snaps can be set globally by using the command **OSNAP** and selecting one or more of the object snap options that have just been described. The command sequence is:

Command:**OSNAP**
Object snap modes:**ENDP,MIDPOI**
Command:

These object snaps will then be in force for all subsequent cursor picks. They can be disabled by using the command

Command:**OSNAP**
Object snap modes:**NONE**
Command:

It is also possible to use a 'running snap'. This is an object snap which is in force while just one entity is picked.

Not only does using object snaps save time, it also ensures that points are picked precisely so that operations such as hatching may be done with no difficulty. Their effective use does require a bit of practice; for instance, it often reduces the number of keystrokes if you can set appropriate object snaps before you enter a drawing command rather than using running snaps during the command. Again, this is a case where **previous planning pays**.

A common problem in computer aided drafting is that it is often needed to pick just one entity from a cluster of several similar ones. This is because some drafters tend to work on too large an area of drawing; this is particularly true of those users experienced in manual drafting, who are prone to regard the screen as a piece of paper. It is possible to use the zoom facility so that the entities can be given more separation and the required one more easily picked. But zooming in and out of drawings takes time. This difficulty can be minimized by using a smaller aperture for picking entities. The size of aperture that you use is a matter of compromise and of personal preference. Too large an aperture and you will have the problem that we have described: too small an aperture increases the required manual precision needed for the pick. In both these cases, speed will suffer. AutoCAD permits you to adjust the size of the aperture box by using the command **APERTURE**. The command sequence is:

Command:**APERTURE**
Object snap target height (1–50 pixels) <10>:**15**
Command:

Setup

In AutoCAD, drawing is done in drawing units, which we can assume to be millimetres, kilometres or light-years. No matter whether we are drawing a pin or a power-station, coordinates are entered directly. In most circumstances, a drawing will eventually be plotted. If we drew the British Isles, we could produce a full size map if we had a large enough plotter (it would be rather difficult to fold, though). It is more usual to plot the drawing to a scale which suits the drafting sheet chosen. This scale can be chosen when the plot is done, but it is better to plan ahead and have a drafting sheet and appropriate scale in mind when the drawing is commenced. This can be done by using the command **SETUP** from the AutoCAD root menu.

The **SETUP** command leads the user through a dialogue. First, the units are established. The choice is made from:

Scientific
Decimal
Engineering
Architectural
Metric

For general engineering purposes, **Metric** is suitable. The user can then pick a scale from a range displayed. The range available depends on the units chosen; for metric units, the range is broadly in line with the standard range shown in Chapter 3. Finally, the user can choose one from a list of sheet sizes. For metric units, the ISO A range is displayed.

When units, scale and sheet size have been chosen, a border is displayed and various variables such as drawing limits, linetype scale and dimension scale are adjusted suitably. The drawn border is not a drafting sheet, it is merely a rectangular box of the precise size of the standard sheet. This border is held as a unit square in a drawing file called 'BORDER.DWG' and is adjusted to the sheet size by **SETUP**.

Exercises

1 Re-draw the form shown in Figure 5.2 using a rotated user coordinate system.

2 Draw the forms shown in Figure 2.8 (page 21), using a snap grid of pitch 5 drawing units.

3 Draw any quadrilateral, join the mid-points of its sides to make another quadrilateral (Figure 5.3a is an example). Demonstrate, using AutoCAD, that this quadrilateral is a parallelogram. (Hint: use **OSNAP** to midpoint of the sides; investigate the **LIST** command to check for parallelism of the sides.)

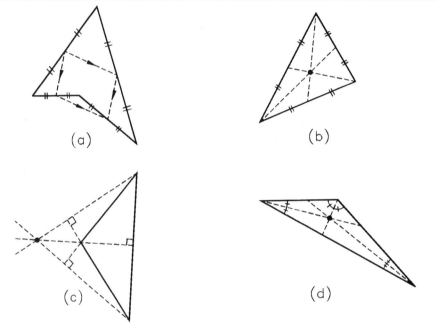

Figure 5.3   Exercise: Object snap

4 Draw any triangle. Demonstrate, using AutoCAD, that the following lines meet at a point:

   (a) The lines joining vertices to the midpoints of their opposite sides (Figure 5.3b).
   (b) The lines from vertices perpendicular to their opposite sides (Figure 5.3c).
   (c) The lines dividing the vertex angles into two (Figure 5.3d).

(Hints. Use **OSNAP** where possible. Exercise (a) is straightforward, (b) and (c) need a little pre-emptive examination of the **EDIT** facilities. If you have problems, leave them and come back to them later. Use **ZOOM** to verify that each set of lines meets at a point.)

6 | Elementary drawing objects

Some of the simpler drawing elements – points, lines, arcs, circles, ellipses and polygons – are introduced. Commands covered are **POINT, LINE, CIRCLE, ARC, POLYGON, ELLIPSE, SOLID** and **DONUT.**

Introduction

Entities are the basic elements which make up drawings; some systems call them 'primitives'. AutoCAD provides a comprehensive set of entities and among these are

Points
Lines
Arcs
Text
Blocks
Attributes
Dimensions
Polylines

In this section we shall be discussing the first three of these.

Before an entity can be placed on a drawing, its position must be defined by coordinates. The number of coordinates depends on the complexity of the entity.

A **point** needs one set of coordinates to define its position.
A **line** needs two sets of coordinates to define its start point and its end point.
An **arc** needs three sets of coordinates to define its start point, an intermediate point and its end point.

These definitions are the simplest; a line could be defined in other ways, for example: its start point, the angle it makes with the X-axis and the Y-coordinate of its endpoint. When drawing, it is convenient, in order to avoid intermediate calculation or geometric construction, to be able to define an entity in alternative ways and AutoCAD provides a good selection.

Lines can be drawn in a continuous chain and, as a special case, AutoCAD provides a separate command for drawing closed polygons. A circle is just a special form of an arc, its subtended angle being 360 degrees. Because circles occur so often in drafting work, there is a special command for drawing them. One might argue that there is a case for treating a circle as a object different from an arc; it has the property of being closed. Due to computer rounding, it is probable that a circle which was a special case of an arc would have a gap, imperceptible on the screen, but numerically real. This might cause trouble in some circumstances, for example, if the geometry were transferred to a computer aided manufacture system which might find it unbounded. It is also convenient to have a command for drawing ellipses; these are approximated by circular arcs and, though they are not entities, can be treated as single objects and moved about the screen as a whole.

Points

Points are the most elementary of entities. They are occasionally of use in drafting when drawings are being laid out and points are planted at the datum points of the different views. A point is drawn by using the command:

Command:**POINT**
Point:**Coordinates**

In order to make a point visible on the display, the system places a blip on the screen. In manual drafting, it is usual to define a point by drawing two short intersecting lines to make it visible. Much the same thing can be done in AutoCAD by using the system variables **PDMODE** and **PDSIZE**.

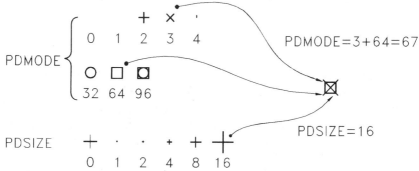

Figure 6.1 PDMODE and PDSIZE

PDMODE governs the format of the mark placed at the point; its settings are:

0	A dot		
1	Nothing	3	A cross (×)
2	A cross (+)	4	A vertical line

In addition, if 32 is added to one of these values, a circle is drawn around the point. If 64 is added, a square is drawn. The results of different settings are shown in Figure 6.1.

PDSIZE, if positive, defines the absolute size of the point figure and, if negative, the size as a percentage of the screen size. **PDMODE** and **PDSIZE** are set by using the command **SETVAR**:

Command:**SETVAR**
Variable name or ?:**PDMODE**
New value for PDMODE <0>:**2**

There are other uses of points in everyday drafting. They are handy for showing data points on curves (Figure 6.2). **PDMODE** = 32 is useful for picking out datum points or characteristic points such as centroids. But, mainly, points are used as nodes which can be snapped to on drawings.

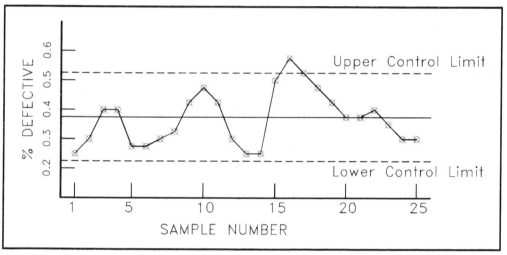

Figure 6.2 PDMODE used to show data points on a curve

Lines

By now, you should be good at drawing with straight lines. There is not much more to add to the remarks made earlier in Chapter 2.

There are responses other than coordinates that can be made in the **LINE** command. In reply to **To point:**, we can input **C**, which closes the chain of lines to make a polygon, if it is possible to close it. If a line has been drawn erroneously, then **U** removes it. This can be repeated right back to the first point input. As we have seen, the **First point:** prompt can be answered by **RETURN**, which results in the last point input being used if the previous command was also **LINE**. If the previous command was **ARC**, which we will deal with next, the endpoint of the last arc becomes the first point of the line and the final tangent direction of the arc becomes the direction of the new line. The line has then been almost fully defined and the prompt changes to **Length of line:** which can be specified. Finally, as has already been mentioned, input of **RETURN** or **SPACE** (known collectively as a **NULL**) in reply to **To point:** quits the command.

Circles

AutoCAD provides five ways of defining a circle. These are:

Centre and radius
Centre and diameter
Three points on the circumference
Two points at the ends of a diameter
Two tangential lines and radius

Command sequences

Centre and radius:

Command:**CIRCLE**
3P/2P/TTR/ < Centre point: > **Specify centre**
Diameter/ < Radius > :**Specify radius**

Centre and diameter:

Command:**CIRCLE**
3P/2P/TTR/ < Centre point: > **Specify centre**
Diameter/ < Radius > :**D**
Diameter:**Specify diameter**

Three points:

Command:**CIRCLE**
3P/2P/TTR/ < Centre point: > **3P**
First point:**Specify point**
Second point:**Specify point**
Third point:**Specify point**

Two points at end of diameter:

Command:**CIRCLE**
3P/2P/TTR/ < Centre point: > **2P**
First point on diameter:**Specify point**
Second point:**Specify point**

Two tangential lines and radius:

Command:**CIRCLE**
3P/2P/TTR/ < Centre point: > **TTR**
Enter tangent spec:**Specify line or circle**
Enter tangent spec:**Specify line or circle**
Radius:**Enter radius**

The options are straightforward, with the exception of **TTR** where a complication is that there may be two possible circles (Figure 6.3a). In this case

AutoCAD makes an informed guess at the user's intention by taking the circle closest to the tangent points specified. There may be no possible circles if the lines are parallel; the command is then aborted. A circle tangential to three circles can be obtained by object snapping to the tangents of the circles. In this case there are even more than two possible circles (How many? See Figure 6.3b).

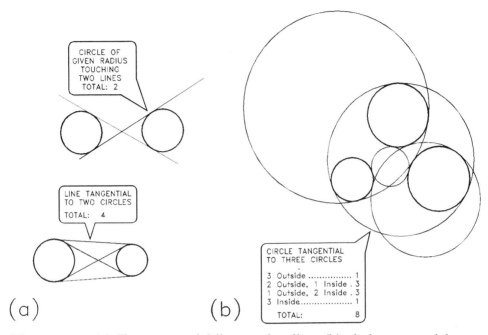

Figure 6.3 (a) Two tangential lines and radius; (b) circles tangential to three circles

Arcs

There are even more ways of drawing an arc than of drawing a circle. The **ARC** sub-menu option shows the eight options in a coded form using:

S   Start point
A   Included angle
C   Centre
D   Start direction
E   Endpoint
L   Chord length
R   Radius

The options are:

The default option, start, intermediate and endpoints
Start point, centre and endpoint (SCE)
Start point, centre and included angle (SCA)
Start point, centre and chord length (SCL)

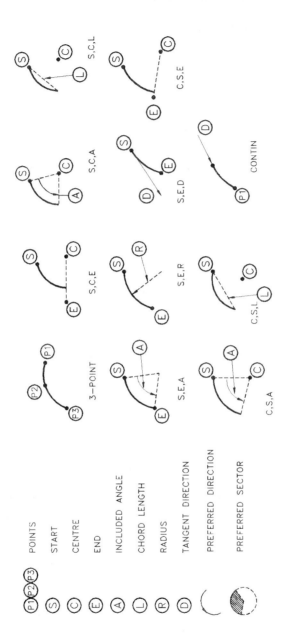

Figure 6.4 Arc options

Start point, endpoint and radius (SER)
Start point, endpoint and included angle (SEA)
Start point, endpoint and start direction (SED)
Continuation of previous line or arc.

The command sequence starts:

Command:**ARC**
Centre/<Start point>:

and continues with prompts depending on the option chosen. If desired, the centre point can be specified first instead of the start point. The options are shown diagrammatically in Figure 6.4. Some comments on the options follow.

(a) Three points (default). This is commonly used to define partially a subsequent arc or line, the continuation start point and direction of the next line or arc being the endpoint and direction of this arc.

(b) SCE. This definition has some redundancy; the endpoint is used only to define the included angle. It is possible to specify the centre first in this case.

(c) SCA. For a positive angle, the arc is drawn anticlockwise.

(d) SCL. There are four possible arcs with a given start point, centre and chord length. AutoCAD resolves this difficulty by using the rule that the arc is drawn in the anticlockwise direction, that a positive chord length denotes the minor arc and that a negative chord length denotes the major arc.

(e) SER. Again four arcs are possible and again the rule is used that the arc is drawn in the anticlockwise direction. A positive radius results in the minor arc being drawn, a negative radius gives the major arc.

(f) SEA. The arc is drawn anticlockwise, a positive angle indicates that the minor arc is to be drawn, a negative angle results in the major arc being drawn.

(g) SED. The start direction can be input by either typing an angle or, more commonly, picking a point in the direction required.

(h) Continuation of previous line or arc. In this case, a **RETURN** is entered at the first prompt. The start point and start direction of the arc are taken to be equal to the endpoint and end direction of the last line or arc defined.

Polygons

This command can be used to draw a regular polygon with up to 1024 sides. The command sequence is:

Command:**POLYGON**
Number of sides:**Input number**
Edge/<Centre of polygon>:

If a point is picked, it is taken as the centre of a base circle for which the radius is requested. The polygon can be either inscribed inside or circumscribed around this base circle. The command continues:

Inscribed in circle/Circumscribed about circle (I/C): **I or C**
Radius of circle:**Specify radius**

If a radius is input by typing its numerical value, the polygon is drawn with one vertex placed at the angle of the snap grid with respect to the centre point. If the radius is picked, a vertex will be placed at the pick point.

Alternatively, the **Edge** option may be used. This will result in the command continuing

First endpoint of edge:**Specify point**
Second endpoint of edge:**Specify point**

Since the number of sides and the length and position of one edge are known, the polygon can be drawn, ambiguity being removed by the usual AutoCAD rule that it is drawn in an anticlockwise direction.

Example. **Polygon and circle**

Brief
Draw the M16 bolt head shown in Figure 6.5a.

Plan of action
The distance across the flats of an M16 bolt head is 24 mm (thread size × 1.5). Use the command **POLYGON** to draw a suitable hexagon, then **CIRCLE** to draw the circle resulting from chamfering the hexagonal bar stock.

Command sequence
Draw the hexagon:

Command:**POLYGON**
Number of sides:**6**
Edge/<centre of polygon>:**Pick the centre**
Inscribed in circle/Circumscribed about circle(I/C):**C**
Radius of circle:**12**

Draw the circle:

Command:**CIRCLE**
3P/2P/TTR/<Centre point>:**TTR**
Enter tangent spec:**Pick side on hexagon**
Enter tangent spec:**Pick side on hexagon**
Radius:**12**

The **TTR** option was selected in order to avoid re-picking the centre of the hexagon.

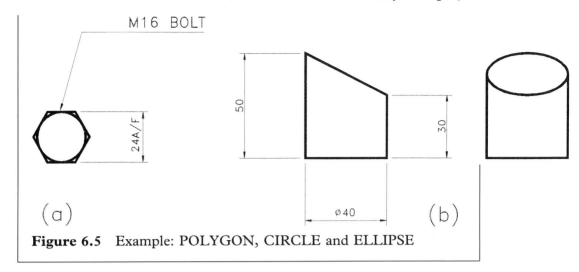

Figure 6.5   Example: POLYGON, CIRCLE and ELLIPSE

Ellipses

An AutoCAD 'ellipse' is an approximation composed of circular arcs. In manual drafting it is usual to construct an ellipse approximately by using four circular arcs (Figure 6.6 shows one method). The AutoCAD construction is a closer approximation, having sixteen circular arcs, and has the useful property that its arcs begin and end at quadrant points.

The ellipse is strictly not a separate entity in its own right but is a closed polyline. Since a polyline *is* an entity, an AutoCAD ellipse can be moved and generally edited as though it were one object. Polylines will be dealt with later; for the moment it is sufficient to note that an ellipse can be split into its

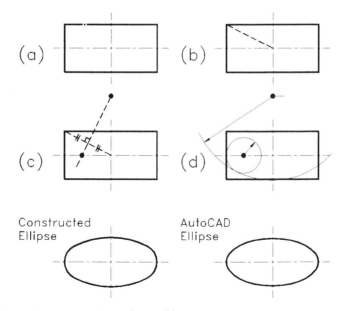

Figure 6.6   Construction of an ellipse

constituent parts by the command **EXPLODE**. These can then be edited like normal arcs. The normal command sequence for drawing an ellipse is:

Command:**ELLIPSE**
< Axis endpoint 1 > /Centre:

but, if isometric snap is enabled, the prompt will be modified in a way which will be described later in Chapter 12. If the default option is selected by specifying a point, the command continues:

Axis endpoint 2:**Specify a point**
< Other axis distance > /Rotation:

Specification of the other axis means that the ellipse is completely defined and so may be drawn. Alternatively, selecting the rotation angle option, by typing **R,** prompts for the input of an angle and the result is an ellipse which is a view of a circle rotated around an axis in the plane of the paper by that angle. This option is very useful in the case of circles in auxiliary views where the angle of the view is known (Figure 6.7).

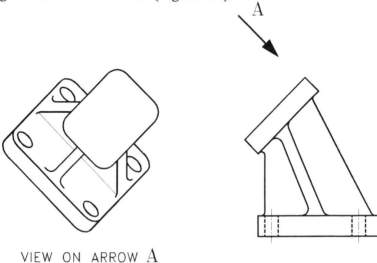

VIEW ON ARROW A

Figure 6.7 Ellipse in auxiliary views

Another way of defining an ellipse is by specifying its centre and its major and minor semi-axes. The command sequence in this case is:

Command:**ELLIPSE**
< Axis endpoint 1 > /Centre:**C**
Centre of ellipse:**Specify centre**
Axis endpoint:**Specify point at end of one axis**
< Other axis distance > /Rotation:**And of other axis**

As may be deduced from the prompt, the rotation angle may also be defined. This has the same effect as that described previously.
Ellipses can be dragged dynamically into position.

Example. **Ellipses**

Brief
Draw the two views of the body shown in Figure 6.5b.

Plan of action
Draw the left hand view using **LINE** and the right hand view using **LINE** and **ELLIPSE**. All coordinates are to be entered relative to the bottom left hand point of the left hand view.

Command sequence
Draw the left hand view:

    Command:**LINE**
    From point:**Pick a point**
    To point:**@0,50**
    To point:**@40,-20**
    To point:**@0,-30**
    To point:**C**

Note that the last coordinate input was **@0,-30**. This will be used to get the relative position of the right hand view. Also, **LINE** will be repeated if **RETURN** is input at the Command: prompt.

    Command:**RETURN**
    From point:**@40,40**
    To point:**@0,-40**
    To point:**@40,0**
    To point:**@0,40**
    To point:**RETURN**

Now draw the ellipse. The last coordinate input was **@0,40**.

    Command:**ELLIPSE**
    <Axis endpoint 1>/Centre:**C**
    Centre of ellipse:**@-20,0**
    Axis endpoint:**@-20,0**
    <Other axis distance>/Rotation:**@0,10**

Apart from being an exercise in relative coordinates, the procedure used has little to recommend it. The right hand view can be constructed much more easily using one of several other methods, the most straightforward being to define a new origin at some convenient point on the view.

Solid figures

Filled-in polygons can be created using the command **SOLID**. The only complication in using this command is in the selection of the polygon's vertices, which must be defined in an order that does not create any overlapping triangles (Figure 6.8). If the vertices are picked in the wrong order, the

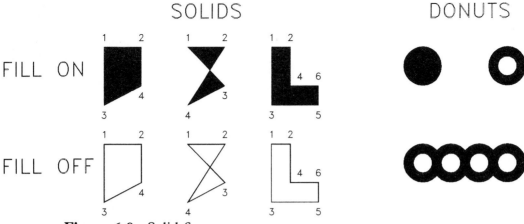

Figure 6.8 Solid figures

result will not be as expected. The polygon will be blocked if the system variable **FILL** is **ON**. If **FILL** is **OFF**, then just the boundary lines will be drawn. There is not much application for **SOLID** in mechanical engineering but it has a use in electronic engineering in the preparation of artwork for printed circuit boards.

Another solid figure is the **DONUT**. This is a circle with thickness. The command sequence is:

Command:**DONUT**
Inside diameter <current value>:**Input I/D**
Outside diameter <current value>:**Input O/D**
Centre of doughnut:**Specify the centre**
Centre of doughnut:**-and another**

. . . .
Centre of doughnut:**RETURN**
Command:

If **FILL** is on, then the doughnut will be filled. If not, then a pair of concentric circles will be drawn. Since **FILL** is a system variable and not a property of the entity, all doughnuts (and all solids) will be filled or all not filled. The reason for permitting **FILL** to be turned off is to reduce temporarily the time taken to draw them on the display. Doughnuts are useful in drafting for various purposes: creating dots at the end of leader lines, drawing attention to datum points, indicating centres of gravity and drawing transverse sections through thin tubes are some examples.

Exercises

1   Draw to scale the shapes shown in Figure 6.9. The pitch of the grid is 10 drawing units.

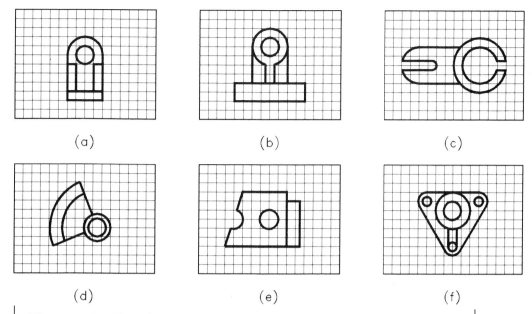

(a)   (b)   (c)

(d)   (e)   (f)

Figure 6.9 Exercise

2 Draw either first or third angle projected drawings of the solids shown in Figure 3.7 (page 31). Take the pitch of the isometric grid as 10 drawing units.

3 Repeat the example on ellipses (above) with the following methods of defining coordinates:
   (a) A snap grid.
   (b) A user coordinate system.

4 Draw the profiled plate shown in Figure 6.10.

PROFILE CONSISTS OF TWO
CIRCULAR ARCS PASSING THROUGH
POINTS A, B, C AND D WITH A
SMOOTH JUNCTION AT POINT C

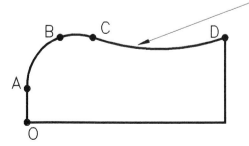

	X	Y
A	0	20
B	20	50
C	40	50
D	120	50

DIMENSIONS RELATIVE TO POINT O

Figure 6.10 Exercise

Editing

This section introduces the powerful AutoCAD facilities for erasing, moving and modifying entities. Commands discussed include **SELECT, ERASE, UNDO, REDO, FILLET, CHAMFER, MOVE, COPY, MIRROR** and **SCALE**.

Selection sets

Many of the extensive set of editing commands that AutoCAD provides act not on a single entity, but on a group of entities – a 'selection set'. A selection set is created by picking entities one at a time or by using a window. An editing command then operates on all the entities in the selection set. On entry to the editing command, the user is first prompted to create a selection set. Alternatively, a selection set can be created in anticipation by using the command **SELECT**. The options in **SELECT** are identical to those embedded in the editing commands. A simple command sequence for **SELECT** is:

Command:**SELECT**
Select objects:**Pick an object**
Select objects:**And another**
. . . .
Select objects:**RETURN**
Command:

References to the selected objects are stored in an editing buffer for further purposes. Objects may be selected singly by specifying coordinates or, more typically, by pointing with the crosshair. In order to simplify object selection, an aperture box is displayed, just as is done in **OSNAP**. But this aperture box is regarded by the system as distinct from the one used in **OSNAP**; its size in pixels is determined by the setting of the system variable **PICKBOX**; you may remember that **APERTURE** is the system variable which holds the size of the **OSNAP** aperture. As with the **OSNAP** aperture, the size is a matter of personal preference.

Although in AutoCAD there is a wide variety of methods of filling selection sets, initially you can manage very well with the default **single object** point option, the **Window** and **Crossing**, the **Undo** and possibly the **Last** options. The action of these options is shown diagrammatically in Figure 7.1.

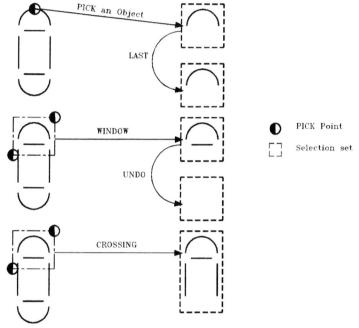

Figure 7.1 Filling selection sets

Point is the option in force when no other option has been chosen. It is used to select one object by cursor or by coordinate input.

Window (W) is used to select a group of objects. The user picks, usually with the cursor, two diagonally opposite corners of a box. All displayed entities which lie entirely within the box are added to the selection set.

Crossing (C) works like **Window**, except that items need not lie wholly in the box. Any object with even the smallest fragment in the crossing box is added to the selection set.

Undo (U) removes the last object, or group of objects, from the selection set.

Last (L) adds the most recently created object to the selection set.

The selection set is created by repeated use of these options. When the set has been completed, the process is terminated by inputting a **RETURN** in response to the prompt 'Select objects:'. As usual, the whole command may be terminated prematurely by **CTRL-C** which has the effect of discarding the objects added to the selection set.

As each object is added to the selection set it is highlighted on the screen, which is useful confirmation of successful selection. More assistance is provided by a message at each selection detailing how many objects have been selected and how many were already selected. In many circumstances, this is a very useful aid to successful editing and you are advised to get into the habit of reading the message.

There are other options that you can investigate when you are comfortable with those shown above. These are **Multiple**, **Box**, **Auto**, **Add**, **Remove**, **Previous** and **Single**. It is stressed again that the majority of users of any computer aided drafting system do not use the whole command set but pick out a sub-set to suit their own preferences and method of working. This is especially true of AutoCAD which has an exceptionally wide range of commands and options.

Erase and undo

At the risk of being considered pessimistic, we would suggest that these commands are the most widely used of all and the more experienced you get the more you will use them, oddly enough. Since correction of errors is such an easy matter on computer aided drafting systems, if you don't make many errors, then you are almost certainly not working fast enough. This also applies to other computer systems such as word processors.

The command **ERASE** is used to remove unwanted objects from the drawing. The command sequence for **ERASE** is:

Command:**ERASE**
Select objects:**Pick object(s) for selection set**
Select objects:**And again**

. . . .
Select objects:**RETURN**

If a set of objects has been erased in error, they can be restored to the drawing by the command **OOPS** which can restore just one **ERASE** (which is normally enough). If you need to cancel the effects of more than one command, it is necessary to use **UNDO**, a generalized form of **U** which we have already met. **UNDO** has the command sequence:

Command:**UNDO**
Auto/Back/Control/End/Group/Mark/<Number>:**Enter number of commands to be undone**
Command:

The most useful is the default option **Number**. When a number is input, that number of commands are undone. **REDO** undoes the **UNDO** so, if you do not know the exact number of commands to be cancelled to get to some previous state, you can use **UNDO**'s and **REDO**'s repeatedly until you find the correct number. In most cases, the number is small and can be established by examining the flip-screen. When you have gained some experience with the use of **UNDO** and **REDO**, then you can investigate the other options.

Fillets and chamfers

Fillets

It is sound engineering practice not to have any sharp corners on a component except in the uncommon case where they are functionally necessary. This is not just for aesthetic or safety reasons; sharp corners often act as stress-raisers on loaded parts. Where two planes intersect, they are usually filleted (in the USA, an external fillet is called a 'round'). In AutoCAD, any two of the entities line, arc and circle can be filleted; a tangential arc is added to the entities, which are trimmed or extended to meet it. As will be seen later, polylines can also be filleted at all nodes in one operation. Before adding a fillet, it is necessary to set the fillet radius, which is done by:

> Command:**FILLET**
> Polyline/Radius/ < Select two lines > :**R**
> Enter fillet radius < current radius > :**Enter radius**
> Command:

The fillet radius can also be set by giving a value to the system variable FILLETRAD, but this is more inconvenient because, from the command sequence above, the **FILLET** command can be used immediately by input of **RETURN**:

> Command:**RETURN**
> Polyline/Radius/ < Select two lines > :**Pick two entities**
> Command:

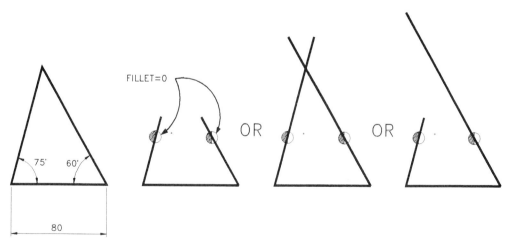

Figure 7.2   Using a fillet of zero radius

A fillet of zero radius is useful for trimming or extending two lines to their intersection point (Figure 7.2 shows how this works). Fillets are also useful for drawing profiles like those shown in Figure 7.3. It is important that fillets and chamfers should be added to a section before it is hatched.

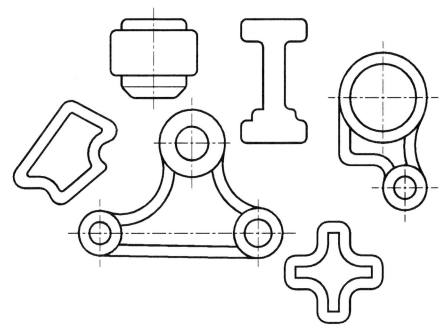

Figure 7.3 Profiles drawn with fillets

Example. Use of the FILLET command

Brief
Add fillets of 10 mm to all marked intersection points of the section shown in Figure 7.4.

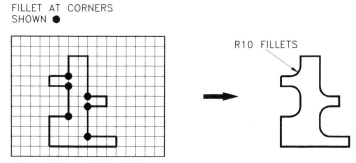

FILLET AT CORNERS
SHOWN ●

R10 FILLETS

Figure 7.4 Use of FILLET

Plan of action
Use **FILLET** firstly to set the fillet radius and secondly to fillet all the relevant entities.

Command sequence
We shall assume that the basic shape has been drawn. Don't forget to use a snap grid, since all the dimensions are multiples of 10 units.

Command:**FILLET**
Polyline/Radius/<Select two lines>:**R**
Enter fillet radius <current radius>:**10**
Command:**RETURN**
Polyline/Radius/<Select two lines>:**Pick pairs of lines to be filleted**

Chamfers

Chamfers are often added to a part for functional reasons, for example to ease the insertion of a piston in a bore. The command **CHAMFER** is used to set the chamfer size and to chamfer two entities in much the same way as **FILLET**.

Command:**CHAMFER**
Polyline/Distance/<Select first line>:**D**
Enter first chamfer distance <Current distance>**Distance**
Enter second chamfer distance <Current distance>**Distance**
Command:**RETURN**
Polyline/Distance/<Select first line>:**Pick line**
Select second line:**Pick the line**
Command:

The order of selecting the lines must correspond with the order in which the relevant chamfer distances were set.

Example. Use of the CHAMFER command

Brief
Add a chamfer to each end of the bore in the part shown in Figure 7.5.

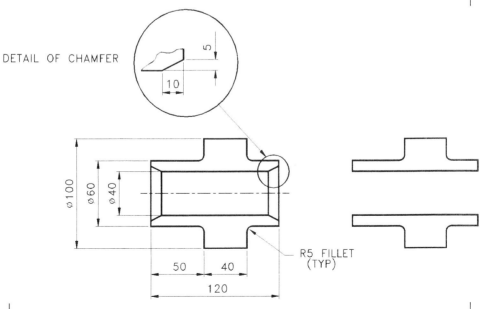

Figure 7.5 Use of CHAMFER

Plan of action
Use the chamfer command firstly to set the chamfer sizes and secondly to perform the chamfer operation.

Command sequence
Draw the form shown on the right hand side of Figure 7.5 using a snap grid of 10 drawing units. You will find it best to draw just the two separated sections at first, as shown. Don't forget to use **FILLET** where possible. Then add the chamfers:

> Command:**CHAMFER**
> Polyline/Distance/<Select first line>:**D**
> Enter first chamfer distance<0.00>:**5**
> Enter second chamfer distance<0.00>:**10**
> Command:**RETURN**
> Polyline/Distance/<Select first line>:**Pick line A**
> Select second line:**Pick line B**
> Command:

Complete the drawing by adding vertical lines so that it looks like the full view on the left.

Since in this case, the chamfer is not the more usual 45 degree type, the order in which the lines are picked is important. The order of specification has been 5 mm then 10 mm. The lines must be picked correspondingly; in this case, the vertical line must be the first picked of the pair of lines to be filleted.

Move and copy

One of the most convenient features of computer aided drafting is the facility of moving or 'dragging' sections of drawings around. In manual drafting, it is common for drawings to be badly placed on the drafting sheet due to bad planning. In AutoCAD, initial placement is not so critical, since it possible to adjust the position of a drawing easily by using the **MOVE** command. **MOVE** is done by filling a selection set with the object to be translated to another position, by picking some reference point (which does not necessarily need to be on the objects to be moved) and then picking the point to which the reference point is to be moved.

The command sequence is:

Command:**MOVE**
Select objects:**Pick selection set**
. . . .
Select objects:**RETURN**
Base point or displacement:**Pick first reference point**
Second point of displacement:**Pick second point**
Command:

Instead of picking a reference point and a second point, a displacement distance can be input as a pair of coordinates in answer to the first point prompt and **RETURN** to the second. Another method is to enter **DRAG** at the first point prompt. The objects can then be visually moved to their destination.

COPY works in much the same way as **MOVE**, except that the original objects are left in place. There is also an option for doing multiple copies. The command sequence for **COPY** is:

Command:**COPY**
Select objects:**Pick selection set**

. . . .
Select objects:**RETURN**
<Base point or displacement>/Multiple:**Pick first reference point**
Second point of displacement:**Pick point to copy to**
Command:

If the option **Multiple** is selected the user is repeatedly prompted for the points at which further copies are to be made.

Example. Use of COPY

Brief
Draw the comb shown in Figure 7.6.

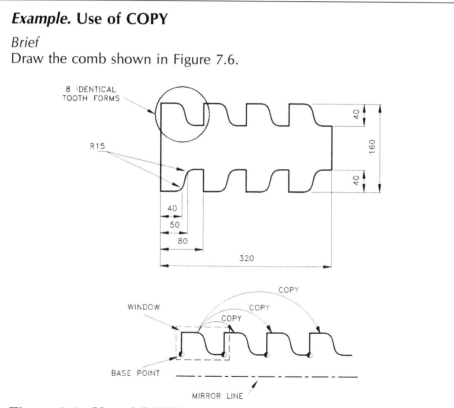

Figure 7.6 Use of COPY

Plan of action
Draw one 'tooth'. Use multiple **COPY** to obtain the full profile. Try to do this *without* using a snap grid, using **OSNAP**s instead. Next, try to **MIRROR** the profile about the centreline. Don't worry if you can't manage it, the **MIRROR** command will be covered next.

Command sequence
Draw the tooth, using **LINE**. **FILLET** to obtain the final tooth form. Now use **COPY**:

Command:**COPY**
Select objects:**W**
First corner:**Pick window as shown in Figure 7.6.**
Second corner:**Complete the window specification.**
Select objects:**RETURN**
<Base point or displacement>/Multiple:**M**
Base point:**Pick as on 7.6 – OSNAP to END of line.**
Second point of displacement:**OSNAP to END of line.**
Second point of displacement:**And to END of new tooth.**
Second point of displacement:**One more time.**
Second point of displacement:**RETURN**

Now try to mirror the form about the horizontal centreline. If you succeed, add the two vertical lines to complete the shape. Note that we needed four **OSNAPS** to the ends of lines. We could have saved ourselves the nuisance of picking the '* * * *' line or pulling down the 'TOOLS' menu four times by planning ahead and setting the **ENDpoint OSNAP** before we entered the **COPY** command.

Mirror

Engineering components often exhibit some degree of symmetry and in such applications the operation **MIRROR** saves a lot of time. It can be used in two ways:

(a) When a form has an axis of symmetry, only half need be drawn; this is then mirrored about the axis to complete the form.
(b) A whole drawing can be mirrored to form the opposite handed component, which is then stored as a separate drawing.

In case (a), the form which has been mirrored is retained; in case (b), the original can be deleted. The command sequence is:

Command:**MIRROR**
Select objects:**Pick selection set**
. . . .
Select objects:**RETURN**
First point of mirror line:**Pick the point**
Second point:**And again**
Delete old objects<N>:**Y or N, depending on application**
Command:

Example. Use of MIRROR

Brief
Draw the component shown in Figure 7.7.

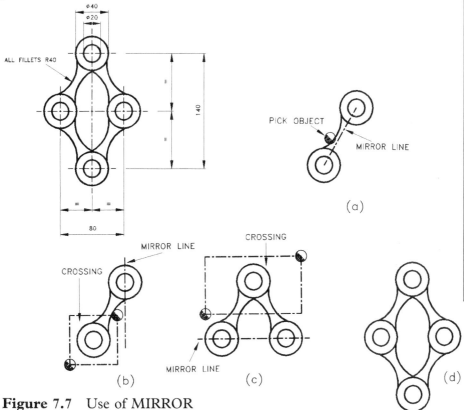

Figure 7.7 Use of MIRROR

Plan of action
Upon examination, it will be noticed that there are three axes of symmetry that can be used to save drafting time. These are shown in Figures 7.7a – 7.7c. Follow the diagram making sure that only the objects to be mirrored are gathered into the selection sets.

Command sequence
Draw the two bosses as in Figure 7.7a. A snap grid of 10 drawing units will be useful. Add the R40 **FILLET**. Now mirror the fillet as shown. You could use **FILLET** a second time but you might as well get into the **MIRROR** mentality as early as possible.

>   Command:**MIRROR**
>   Select objects:**Pick the fillet.**
>   Select objects:**RETURN**
>   First point of mirror line:**Pick centre of boss**
>   Second point of mirror line:-**and the other centre.**
>   Delete old objects< N >:**RETURN**

> The remainder of the drawing is completed similarly, the only difference being that a crossing box is used for the selection of objects.
>
> *Note.* Notice that in none of the mirroring operations is any object mirrored onto itself. This may not seem to be important at the moment, since even if we do mirror an object onto itself it will not show on the display. But if we were to plot the drawing later on a pen plotter, then the superimposed object would be drawn twice and would very likely appear to have been drawn in a thicker line than the other objects on the drawing.

Scale

The command **SCALE** first requires a selection set, then a base point and a scale factor. The selection set is scaled by the factor about the base point. The scale factor is greater than one for the selection set to be expanded and less than one for the selection set to be contracted. All points of the selection set will be displaced except the base point – which is the centre of the scaling. The command sequence is:

Command:**SCALE**
Select objects:**Pick selection set**
. . . .
Select objects:**RETURN**
Base point:**Pick point**
<Scale factor>/Reference:**Input scale factor**
Command:

The Reference option requires that a reference length should be input, together with a size to which that length should be altered.

> ### *Example.* Use of SCALE
>
> *Brief*
> Figure 7.8 shows a wire clip of diameter 4 mm. Design and draw a range of three clips from 5 mm to 10 mm.
>
> *Plan of action*
> It is not usually ideal to design a range in which dimensions increase in arithmetic progression; a geometric progression is better. Items such as electric light bulbs, fuses and resistors have ranges which conform to this principle. In this case, the ratio between the smallest and largest items is 2. The middle item will be in a ratio of the square root of 2, or approximately 1.4. The scale factors are then 1, 1.4, 2. Such calculations occur so often in detail design that there are several helpful standards available. A useful publication is PD 6481, published by the British Standards Institution.

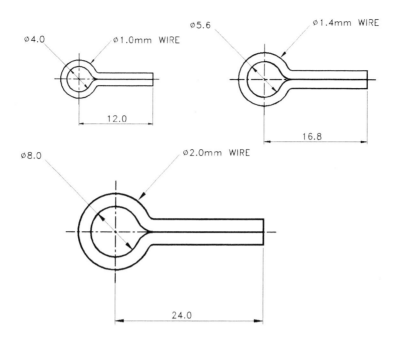

Figure 7.8   Use of SCALE

Command sequence
Assuming that the smallest clip has been drawn, we proceed as follows:

Command:**COPY**
Select objects:**W**
First point:**Pick a window surrounding the whole clip**
Second point: **– complete the specification**
Select objects:**RETURN**
<Base point or displacement>/Multiple:**M**
Base point:**Pick a handy point – the centre will do**
Second point of displacement:**Position of the next**
Second point of displacement:**-and the next.**
Second point of displacement:**RETURN**
Command:

It is as well to space the clips out well, since we shall be scaling them.

Command:**SCALE**
Select objects:**W**
First point:**Pick a window round the second clip**
Second point:**Finish the specification**
Select objects:**RETURN**
Base point:**Pick the leftmost point of the second clip**
<Scale factor>/Reference:**1.4**

Repeat with the third clip but use a scaling factor of 2.

Offset

OFFSET is a command which has frequent application in engineering drawing. It draws an entity parallel with another, specified, entity at a defined distance from it. The offset distance may be defined directly or may be specified by indicating a point that the offset must pass through. The command sequence is:

Command:**OFFSET**
Offset distance or Through <last distance>:**Input distance**
Select object to offset:**Pick the object**
Side to offset:**Pick point on the desired side**
Command:

If the option **Through** has been selected, then the last prompt will be:

Through point:**Pick point through which offset will pass**

Example. Use of OFFSET

Brief
Draw the cast shell shown in Figure 7.9.

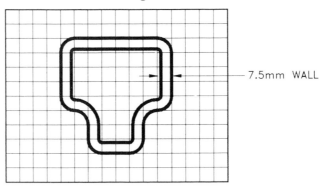

Figure 7.9 Use of OFFSET

Plan of action
Draw half the form and offset each entity by 7.5 mm towards the inside of the form. Mirror to obtain the whole part.

Command sequence
Assuming that the half section has been drawn;

Command:**OFFSET**
Offset distance or Through <0>:**7.5**
Select object to offset:**Pick the top line**
Side to offset:**Pick point below line**
Command:**RETURN**
Offset distance or Through <7.5>:**RETURN**
Select object to offset:**Pick the top radius**
Side to offset:**Pick point inside arc**
Command:**RETURN**

And so on.

This exercise could have been done much more quickly if the profile had been defined by a polyline. You can repeat it later when we have described how to define polylines.

Exercises

1   Draw the forms shown in Figure 7.10. You will find **COPY** useful.

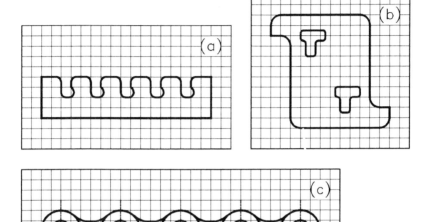

Figure 7.10   Exercise: COPY

2   Using the command **MIRROR**, draw the shapes shown in Figure 7.11.

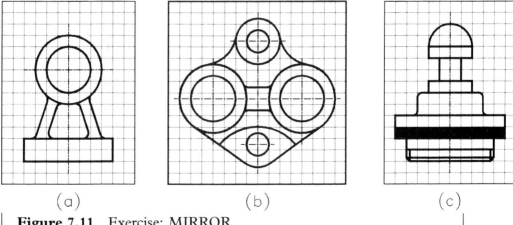

(a)   (b)   (c)

Figure 7.11   Exercise: MIRROR

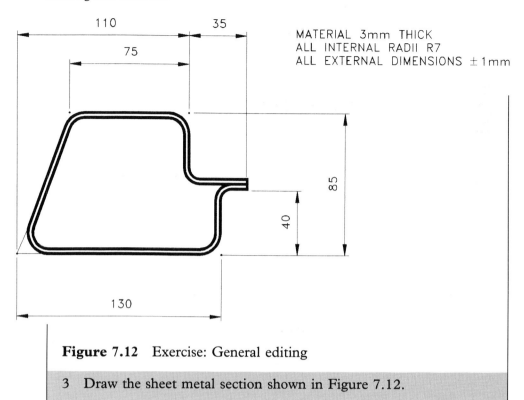

MATERIAL 3mm THICK
ALL INTERNAL RADII R7
ALL EXTERNAL DIMENSIONS ±1mm

Figure 7.12 Exercise: General editing

3   Draw the sheet metal section shown in Figure 7.12.

8 More editing

A further set of editing commands is discussed. This includes **ROTATE, BREAK, TRIM, EXTEND, STRETCH, ARRAY, CHANGE, DIVIDE** and **MEASURE.** The **INQUIRY** commands are also covered.

Rotate

Objects can be rotated about a point by using the command **ROTATE**. The command sequence is:

Command:**ROTATE**
Select objects:**Pick selection set**

. . . .
Select objects:**RETURN**
Base point:**Pick centre of rotation**
< Rotation angle >/Reference:**Input angle in degrees**

The positive direction of rotation is, as usual in AutoCAD, anticlockwise. If the **Reference** option is selected, then the system expects the angle not in explicit form but as the angle of an existing object and the angle to which it is to be rotated. This is useful when the rotation angle is not known directly and would require calculation. The reference angle may be input indirectly by pointing to the two endpoints of an existing line and then the new angle can be specified.

Example. **Use of ROTATE**

Brief
Rotate the form shown in Figure 8.1 so that the side AB is horizontal.

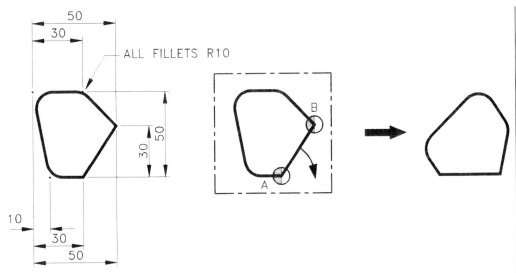

Figure 8.1 Use of ROTATE

Plan of action
The angle between AB and the horizontal is arctan(30/20). The required angle of rotation is then 56.310 degrees in a clockwise direction.

Command sequence
Draw the form shown in Figure 8.1. Then rotate it into position as follows:

> Command:**ROTATE**
> Select objects:**W**
> First corner:**Pick lower left corner**
> Other corner:**Pick upper right corner**
> Select objects:**RETURN**
> Base point:**Pick point A**
> <Rotation angle>/Reference:**-56.310**
> Command:

In this case, the calculation is admittedly minor, but it is not always so. It is easier (and better practice) to let the computer perform calculations whenever possible, since the likelihood of a mistake is lower and also the result will be to the maximum possible accuracy. A better sequence would be:

> Command:**ROTATE**
> Select objects:**W**
> First corner:**Pick lower left corner**
> Other corner:**Pick upper right corner**
> Select objects:**RETURN**
> <Rotation angle>/Reference:**R**
> Reference angle:**Pick point A**
> Second point:**Point B, using Osnap to END**
> New angle:**0**
> Command:

Break

Often, in building up a drawing, it is necessary to erase a section of an entity between two points. The command to do this is **BREAK**:

Command:**BREAK**
Select object:**Pick object to be broken**
Enter first point:**Pick one point of the break**
Enter second point:**Pick point at other end of the break**
Command:

If the object is selected by pointing, rather than by windowing, then the pick point is assumed to be the first point of the break, but the system checks by returning:

Enter second point (or F for first point):

Entry of **F** results in AutoCAD prompting for the first, then second, points of the break as previously shown. This is a necessary option because very often a break point is at the intersection of two or more entities and, in order correctly to specify the object to be broken, it must be picked at a location remote from the break point (and the intersection). The second break point need not be precisely on the entity since a point on the entity nearest to the pick point is chosen automatically.

BREAK is a versatile command and can be used to divide an entity into two sections by picking identical break points. It can be used to trim an entity by specifying one of the break points at the end of the entity. It is important to remember that when a break is made in an arc or a circle, the resulting gap is anticlockwise from first to second break points – in other words, in the positive direction. This is very easily forgotten but, if the break is not satisfactory, remedial action can be taken by using **U** to remove the effect of the previous command.

Example. **Use of BREAK**

Brief
Draw the shape shown in Figure 8.2a.

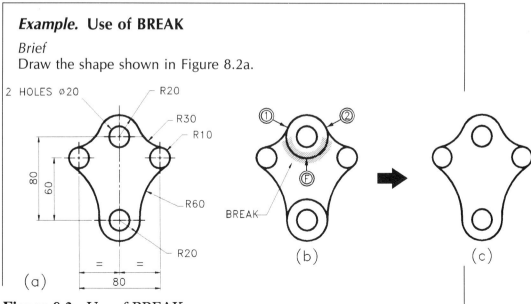

Figure 8.2 Use of BREAK

Plan of action
First, draw the six full circles and use **FILLET** to complete the profile. The larger circles will not be trimmed back to the fillet and so they must be broken. A convenient **OSNAP** is the end of the fillet arcs, so, in order to specify that it is the circles that are to be broken and not the fillet, it is necessary to use the **F** option in **BREAK**.

Command sequence
Draw the form shown in Figure 8.2b. The shaded portion is to be removed from the upper circle.

Command:**BREAK**
Select object:**Pick point at F on Figure 8.2b**
Enter second point (or F for first point):**F**
Enter first point:**OSNAP to end of fillet – point 1**
Enter second point:**OSNAP to end of fillet – point 2**
Command:

Continue, breaking the lower circle in similar fashion. The result should look like Figure 8.2c.

Trim

The **BREAK** command can be used to truncate an entity by specifying a break point at the end of the entity, but the **TRIM** command can do this in rather a more particularized way. Using this command, one or more entities are broken at one or more cutting edges.

▼ TRIM LINE
o OBJECTS TO TRIM

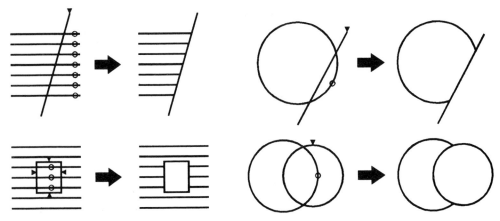

Figure 8.3 Use of TRIM

A command sequence is:
Command:**TRIM**
Select cutting edges ...
Select objects:**Pick a selection set**
. . . .
Select objects:**RETURN**
Select object to trim:**Pick an object**
. . . .
Select object to trim:**RETURN**
Command:

Some examples of the use of **TRIM** are shown in Figure 8.3. There are a few restrictions on trimming, but these are all commonsense and will not be discussed further.

Extend

The action of **EXTEND** is opposite to that of **TRIM**; selected objects may be extended to meet existing boundary edges. The command sequence is:

Command:**EXTEND**
Select boundary edge(s)...
Select objects:**Pick selection set**
. . . .
Select objects:**RETURN**
Select object to extend: **Pick object**
. . . .
Select object to extend:**RETURN**
Command:

Some examples are shown in Figure 8.4.

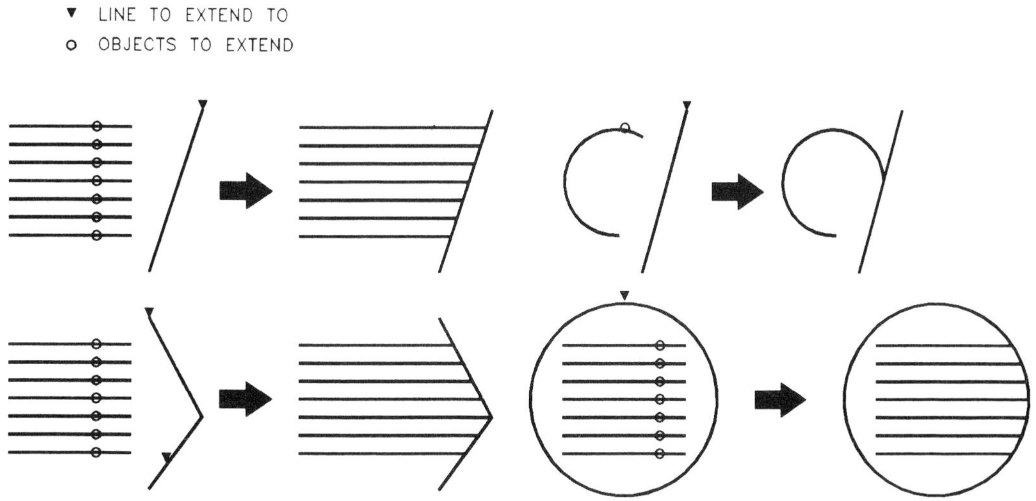

▼ LINE TO EXTEND TO
o OBJECTS TO EXTEND

Figure 8.4 Use of EXTEND

Stretch

Although it is just as easy to use, the action of the **STRETCH** command is rather more complex than that of **EXTEND**. If a detail of a drawing is stretched, then it is moved but its connexions to other parts of the drawing are still maintained. The objects to be moved are specified, often by using a crossing box (see the notes on **SELECT** in Chapter 7 if you need reminding about crossing boxes). Then the translation is defined by a base point and the new point to which the base point must move. The objects are moved to their new positions and all entities which connect with them are extended so that the topology of the drawing is maintained although its dimensions are not.

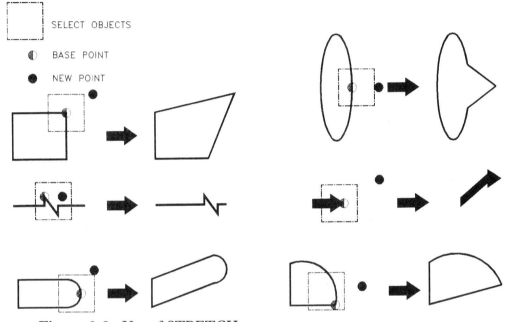

SELECT OBJECTS

BASE POINT

NEW POINT

Figure 8.5 Use of STRETCH

The command acts like a combination of **MOVE** and **EXTEND**. The command sequence is:

Command:**STRETCH**
Select objects to stretch by window . . .
Select objects:**C**
First corner:**Pick bottom left corner of box**
Other corner:**Pick top right corner of box**

. . . .
Select objects:**RETURN**
Base point:**Pick reference point on objects to stretch**
New point:**Pick point to move base point**
Command:

Sometimes, the action of **STRETCH** is a little unexpected. All the results can be explained if you bear in mind that the command acts, not on entities, but on *definition points*. Each type of entity is defined by a set of values: a straight line by the coordinates of its endpoints, for instance. When one endpoint is selected in a **STRETCH**, it is moved: if the other is not selected, then it is anchored in its original position.

Some examples are shown in Figure 8.5.

Array

The **ARRAY** command is important because, in the correct circumstances, it is a great time saver. It is a generalization of the **COPY** command since it is used to make multiple copies of a form in either a rectangular pattern or arranged around a circle. The initial command sequence is as follows:

Command:**ARRAY**
Select objects:**Pick selection set**

. . . .
Select objects:**RETURN**
Rectangular or Polar array:(R/P)

If the **Rectangular** (or **R** option) is chosen, the user is asked for the numbers of rows and columns that are to be used in the rectangular pattern. In this context, the usual mathematical convention is observed: that rows are in a horizontal direction and columns in a vertical. The distances between the rows and columns are then requested and again the mathematical convention applies, that distances to the right and upwards are positive, and distances to the left and down are negative. Alternatively, the diagonal corners of a unit cell may be supplied. The command sequence then continues:

Rectangular or Polar array:(R/P):**R**
Number of rows(–––)<1>:**Input number**
Number of columns(| | |)<1>:**Input number**
Unit cell or distance between rows(–––):**Input distance**
Distance between columns(| | |):**Input distance**
Command:

If the **Unit cell** option is chosen, the array has been completely defined and no further information is required (or requested). A rectangular array at an angle to the horizontal can be generated easily by using the **Rotate** option in **SNAP** and rotating the grid to the desired angle before using the **ARRAY** command.

If the **Polar** (or **P**) option is chosen, the user is prompted for the centre point of the circular array, then the total number of items which will be drawn in the polar array, the total angle which is to be used for the array and the angle between each element. The astute reader may have noticed that these inputs would result in an over-determined array. This is so, and not all the responses are needed. The array may be determined by any two of (a) the number of items, (b) the total angle, (c) the angle between adjacent items – **RETURN** being returned to a redundant prompt. The system is clever enough to adjust the command sequence to suit the previous inputs. The command sequence continues:

Number of items:
Angle to fill ($+ =$CCW, $- =$CW):

If both of these are supplied, the array will be drawn. If the number of items has been input and **RETURN** returned for the angle, then the sequence continues:

Angle between items ($+ =$CCW, $- =$CW):

If the number of items is not specified, then the direction of the array has already been defined by the signed angle in response to the 'Angle to fill' prompt; continuation is:

Angle between items:

The final piece of information needed is:

Rotate objects as they are copied? $<$Y$>$:

The procedure, like many in AutoCAD, sounds rather more difficult than it is in practice.

Example. **Use of ARRAY**

Brief
Create a drawing of the component shown in Figure 8.6.

Plan of action
The hole pattern is a combination of rectangular and polar arrays. First, draw one hole – say the topmost one. Next use a rectangular array of four rows and one column to obtain one pattern of four holes. Finally, use a polar array, filling 360 degrees with sixteen items.

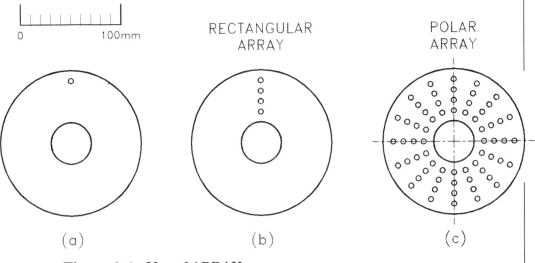

0   100mm

RECTANGULAR
ARRAY

POLAR
ARRAY

(a)   (b)   (c)

Figure 8.6 Use of ARRAY

Command sequence
Draw the view shown in Figure 8.6a. Then create a rectangular array of holes with four rows and one column:

Command:**ARRAY**
Select objects:**Pick the lone circle**
Select objects:**RETURN**
Rectangular or Polar array (R/P):**R**
Number of rows(– – –)<1>:**4**
Number of columns(| | |)<1>:**RETURN**
Unit cell or distance between rows(– – –):**-10**)

The drawing should now look like Figure 8.6b.

Command:**RETURN**
Select objects:**W**
First corner:**Pick corner**
Other corner:**Opposite corner**
Select objects:**RETURN**
Rectangular or Polar array (R/P):**P**
Number of items:**16**
Angle to fill (+ =CCW, – =CW)<360>:**RETURN**

The drawing should now look like Figure 8.6c

Change

Often, the properties of an existing entity are not what is required. It is possible to modify them by using the command **CHANGE**. The command sequence is:

Command:**CHANGE**
Select objects:**Pick selection set**

. . . .
Select objects:**RETURN**
Properties/<Change point>:

If the **Properties** option is selected by input of **P**, an opportunity is given to change any of the following entity properties:

The colour of an entity.
The linetype of an entity.
The layer on which an entity is placed.
The thickness of a polyline.

If **RETURN** is returned then it is assumed that the entity to be changed is text.

If the **Change point** option is selected (by default) then various actions can take place, depending on the type of the entity:

• If it is a line, its nearest endpoint will be moved to the input point.
• If it is a circle, its radius will change so that the circle passes through the input point.

- If it is text, then its style, height, rotation angle and message can be altered.
- If it is a block, its position can be altered.

The properties of text and blocks will be dealt with later.

Divide and measure

DIVIDE is a command that is often useful in construction. It marks an entity at a fixed number of equally spaced spans.

Command:**DIVIDE**
Select object to divide:**Pick just one entity**
<Number of segments>/Block:

If a whole number is entered, marks are added at equally spaced points. If **Block** is selected, then the name of a previously defined block will be requested, and this will be used for the marker. The block can be aligned with the object, if desired. The command continues in this case:

Block name to insert:
Align block with object?<Y>:
Number of segments:

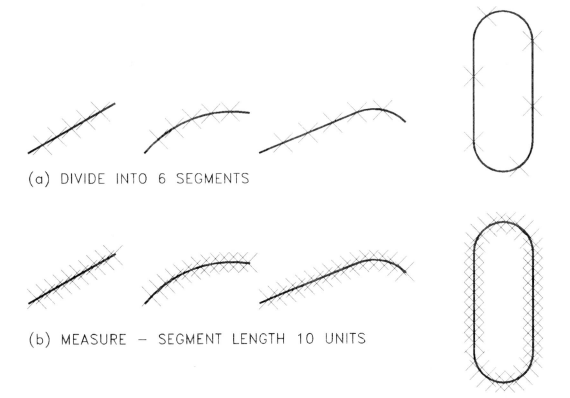

(a) DIVIDE INTO 6 SEGMENTS

(b) MEASURE — SEGMENT LENGTH 10 UNITS

Figure 8.7 Use of DIVIDE and MEASURE

MEASURE is the operation inverse to **DIVIDE**. It places markers along an entity at fixed intervals.

Command:**MEASURE**
Select object to measure:**Pick just one entity**
<Segment length>/Block:

If a segment length is defined, markers are placed along the entity the specified length apart. If **Block** is picked, the continuation is precisely the same as with **DIVIDE**. Examples of **DIVIDE** and **MEASURE** are shown in Figure 8.7.

The remaining commands in this section are not really editing commands; they are 'inquiries'. They are included here for convenience.

Inquiry commands

The **LIST** command allows one to choose a selection set and list the properties of the entities contained in it.

DBLIST produces a list of the properties of *all* the entities in a drawing. It is seldom useful since it produces so much information. The information can, however, be listed on a printer

ID returns the coordinates of a point that is picked.

DIST returns the distance and angle between two specified points.

AREA returns the area and perimeter of a defined form. If the form is not closed, then the system closes it. The figure can be made up from lines, and can have holes inside. Boundaries can be added or subtracted to derive the total area.

Example. **Use of AREA**

Brief
Figure 8.8a shows a shape that is to be pressed from steel strip and the nesting schedule for its manufacture. Find the percentage utilization for the layout shown in Figure 8.8d, if there must be at least 10 mm space between each neighbouring shape and 5 mm space to the edge of the strip.

Plan of action
Since there must be at least 10 mm separation, this can be regarded *approximately* as a 5 mm offset around each form. This also accounts for the edge clearance. Draw one complete sequence from centreline to centreline. Using **AREA**, find the area of strip required for the sequence and subtract from it the areas of the two half patterns.

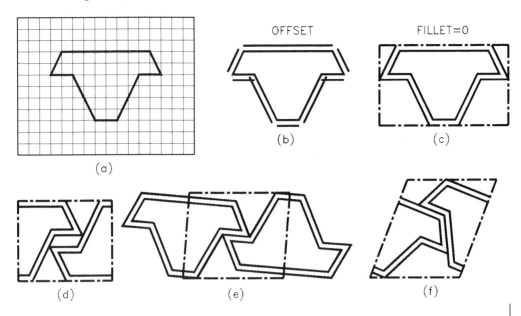

Figure 8.8 Use of AREA

Command sequence
Draw the form shown in Figure 8.8a. **OFFSET** it to establish a 5 mm border (Figure 8.8b). The offset lines will be disjoint but can be made continuous by filleting them in pairs with a zero fillet (Figure 8.8c). A rectangle representing the piece of the strip which will hold one pressing is drawn. For clarity in the illustration, the rectangle is shown in a different line style from the pressing, but this is unnecessary. Next find the areas of the pressing (without 5 mm allowance) and the rectangle which will enclose the pressing (with the 5 mm allowance). The ratio between these is the material utilization.

Command:**AREA**
< First point >/Entity/Add/Subtract:**Hit a point on the rectangle**
Next point:**and the next, traversing the perimeter**
Next point:**and so on**

. . . .
Next point:**RETURN**
Area = 8132.62, Perimeter = 372.36

Now do the same thing with the inner form, traversing the perimeter and indicating that the boundary is complete by entering **RETURN**. You may find that using **OSNAP** to snap to intersection points is useful. You should get an answer of 3400. The percentage material utilization is about 41.8%.

Figures 8.8d–f show other nesting arrangements. A more accurate answer would be obtained by using, not a zero fillet, but a 5 mm fillet so that the form was rounded at the two sharp points.

Exercises

1   Reproduce some of the examples shown in Figures 8.3, 8.4, 8.6 and 8.7.

2   Repeat the example on **AREA**, above, but using the other nesting layouts. Which gives the best material utilization?

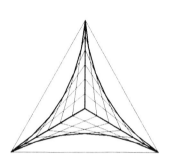   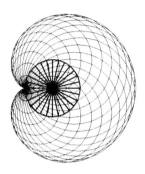   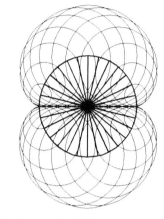

(a) DELTOID   (b) CARDIOID   (c) CYCLOID

Figure 8.9   Exercise: Editing

3   Draw the three constructions in Figure 8.9.
   (a) use **DIVIDE** to mark off the lines.
   (b) use **ARRAY** to mark off the base circle.
   (c) use **DIVIDE** to mark off the base circle.

9 Linetypes and layers

A discussion of the different styles of lines used in engineering drafting and how they are provided in AutoCAD. Layers in drafting, their advantages and implementation. Commands covered include **LAYER** and **LTSCALE**.

Introduction

A powerful aid to communication in drafting is the use of different kinds of lines to represent different kinds of objects. There are well-established conventions for the use of these linetypes (or 'line fonts'). AutoCAD supplies the standard linetypes shown in Figure 9.1.

Not all of the AutoCAD linetypes are useful in engineering drafting but the three which are prefixed by an asterisk are standard in general drafting practice. Each is used conventionally to convey special information about the part being drawn and it is recommended that you should only use these.

In addition, there are two conventional linetypes which do not come with AutoCAD but which are commonly used in drafting. These are also shown in Figure 9.1. If you wish to use either of them, then you must draw them manually.

In engineering standards such as BS 308, not only are different styles of lines recommended, but also different line thicknesses. In the drawings that you have been doing, using **LINE**, **CIRCLE** and similar drawing commands, all the objects will have been displayed on the screen in the same thickness. There is no way, using these commands, that lines can be shown in differential thicknesses. In practice, if you are using a multi-pen plotter with liquid ink pens, then there is no difficulty in obtaining different line thicknesses; different pen widths can be used and allocated to the linetypes. As we will see later, thicker lines can also be displayed and plotted using polylines.

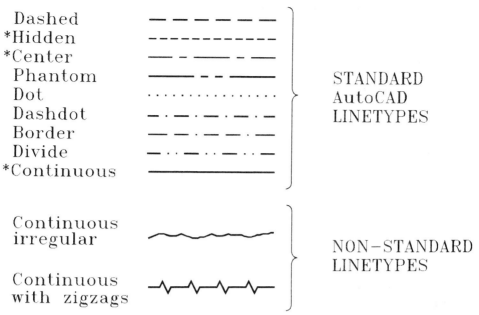

Figure 9.1 Standard linetypes

Standard line thicknesses

In Chapter 3 it was mentioned that the ISO recommendation for drafting sheets was based on the principle that all sheets should have a constant narrow/long side ratio of $1:\sqrt{2}$, the form of a sheet being obtained by halving the next larger sheet along the wider side. There is a standard (ISO 3098/1) for line thicknesses which follows the same principle. The range of line thicknesses recommended are:

0.13, 0.18, 0.25, 0.35, 0.5, 0.7, 1.0, 1.4, 2.0.

In this series, each line thickness is approximately $\sqrt{2}$ times the previous thickness. They are the familiar DIN series of liquid pen sizes.

The use of these standard line thicknesses means that if the thickness is matched to the sheet size, the lines will still be standard for any standard scale of reproduction. It is recommended that the following combinations of drafting sheet and line thickness should be used:

A0   1.4,   1.0,   0.7
A1   1.0,   0.7,   0.5
A2   0.7,   0.5,   0.35
A3   0.5,   0.35, 0.25
A4   0.35, 0.25, 0.18
A5   0.25, 0.18, 0.13

Again, we would stress that it is a mistake to stick to a standard rigidly; the prime aim of a piece of drafting is to communicate. If an off-standard line thickness aids communication, then use it.

93

Standard linetypes and their uses

Continuous linetype

So far we have used continuous lines exclusively. Two widths of continuous line are recommended in standards and are used as follows:

Thin continuous lines   Fictitious lines
                                   Dimensions, projection and leader lines
                                   Hatching
Thick continuous lines   Visible outlines and edges

Examples of the use of continuous lines are shown in Figure 9.2.

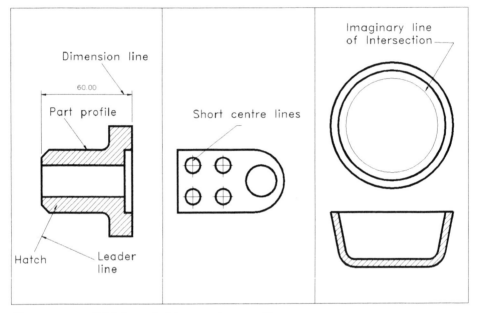

Figure 9.2   Thick and thin continuous lines

Long chain linetype

Thin long chain lines   Centrelines
                                Pitch circle lines
                                Parts in front of cutting planes
Thick long chain lines   Cutting planes
                                Surfaces for special treatment

Chain lines are used mainly to indicate symmetry. There are some rules of good practice in their use.

  (a) Centrelines should extend a short distance beyond the feature they apply to.
  (b) Centrelines should not be drawn continuously from one view to another.

(c) Centrelines should start and finish with a long dash.

(d) Intersecting centrelines should cross on a line and not on a gap.

The observance of rules (a) and (b) is within the control of the user. Rule (c) is observed automatically by AutoCAD. Rule (d) is difficult to comply with on computer aided drafting systems in general. We would recommend that, where possible, you should follow Rules (a) and (b). AutoCAD will follow Rule (c) for you. Forget Rule (d).

The mark-space ratios for the linetypes supplied with AutoCAD and shown in Figure 9.1 are perfectly satisfactory and accord with examples shown in standards such as BS 308. If they do not suit your particular application, then there is a facility for defining your own customized line-type; this should rarely be necessary. BS 308 suggests that, for long centrelines, the relative lengths of the dashes should be increased. This, presumably to reduce drawing time, is unnecessary in computer aided drafting.

Where centrelines are very short, for example on small holes, it is preferable to use thin continuous lines rather than chain lines.

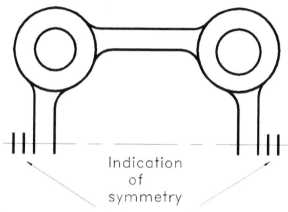

Figure 9.3 Parts symmetrical about an axis

When parts are symmetrical about an axis, they need not be drawn fully (Figure 9.3). Notice that symmetry is indicated by using pairs of short parallel lines at the ends of the chain lines. Notice also that the profile is drawn slightly overlapping the axis of symmetry. Since mirroring about an axis is done so easily in AutoCAD, this device should be used sparingly and only when space is extremely tight.

Examples of the use of chain lines are shown in Figure 9.4.

Short dash linetype

Thin short dash lines   Crests of hidden threads.
Thick short dash lines   Hidden outlines and edges.

The main use of dash lines is to indicate profiles that are obscured by the material of the component in the view being drawn. Just as with chain lines, there are some points of style which are used in manual drafting and which

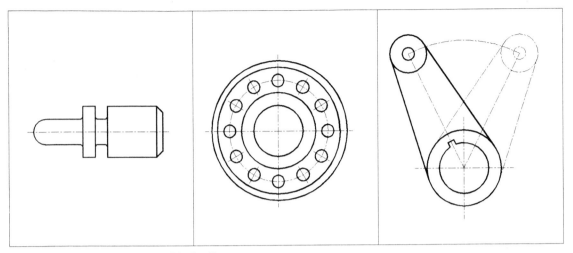

Figure 9.4   Chain lines

are applicable also to computer aided drafting. Mostly, they are catered for by AutoCAD but there is one which is controlled by the drafter. Very often, in the interests of clarity, it is best to omit some of the hidden lines which would be drawn if we were merely interested in strict geometric accuracy. It is a temptation for inexperienced drafters to show all possible hidden lines on a drawing. Again, it must be remembered that the engineering drawing is primarily a vehicle of communication and that drafters are entitled to use any means at all to help visualization of the part being drawn. Figure 9.5 shows a very simple case in which inclusion of all the possible hidden lines in the right hand view would lead to confusion.

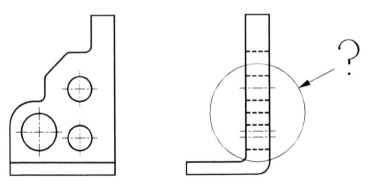

Figure 9.5   Hidden lines

Continuous freehand lines

These are used for limits of partial views and sections where the part line does not fall on an axis.

The linetype is not supplied with with AutoCAD, but can easily be drawn using the **SKETCH** option. An example is shown in Figure 9.6.

There are also two linetypes which are not included in most standards but which should be mentioned.

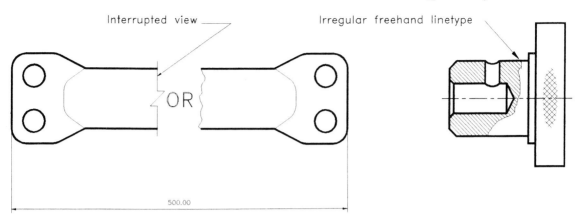

Figure 9.6   Continuous freehand lines

Continuous lines with zigzags

These are used in the same way as continuous freehand lines for interrupting views of long regular components where space is tight. They are commonly found and look neater than continuous freehand lines but, since they are not standard in AutoCAD and are more troublesome to draw, they are best avoided unless you prefer them strongly. An example of their use is also shown in Figure 9.6.

Construction lines

When a drawing is being laid out by a manual drafter, it is the usual practice to use faint construction lines which are subsequently erased from the final

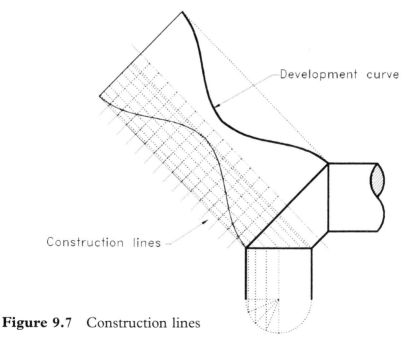

Figure 9.7   Construction lines

drawing. Construction lines are used in such applications as positioning views and drawing intersection curves (Figure 9.7). Since they do not appear on the final drawing, there is no standard for their style. They are useful in computer aided drafting and it is usual to use some method of distinguishing them from lines which are permanent. So that they may be distinguished on both colour and monochrome screens, we shall adopt the purely arbitrary convention that they will be drawn using the AutoCAD **DOT** linetype and in a special colour. We shall see later in this chapter how this is achieved.

Layer utilization

It has been mentioned earlier that AutoCAD drawings can be organized as a series of layers (Figure 9.8). Using layers is like drawing on a pad of super-imposed transparencies, each of which can be made visible or invisible. It is good practice to organize even a simple drawing into layers; for complex drawings, it is a necessity. Commonly, installations provide a standard schedule for layer utilization, each layer being used for a separate purpose. Later on in this chapter, we shall develop our own layer schedule.

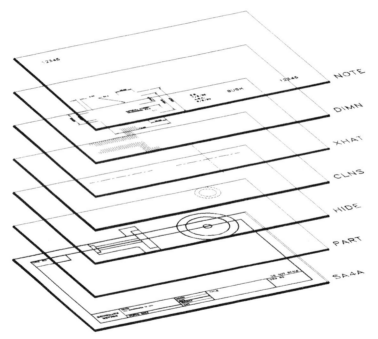

Figure 9.8 Layers

Layered drawings are useful because of the degree of flexibility that they provide. Some reasons for their use are:

(a) Working on separate layers can reduce regeneration time in AutoCAD.
(b) Construction lines can be drawn on a separate layer and removed quickly.

(c) Alternative forms of drawing can be generated – for example, alternative dimensions (metric and imperial), German and English notes and alternative material specifications.

(d) Drawings can be made with subsets of layers being grouped for special purposes – for example, details of manufacture can be removed easily when drawings are to be supplied to customers.

(e) Alternative dimensioning systems can be used. Thus, one drawing might show functional dimensions, another might show manufacturing dimensions and a third, gauging dimensions.

(f) In installations that have only a single-pen plotter, plotting can be done selectively by layers, so that drawings using different colours and linetypes can be prepared.

In AutoCAD, layers when they are created are given a name by the user. It is good practice to give the layer a name which is easily associated with its use. For instance, one of our standard layers is to hold an A4 drawing sheet. We shall call it SA4A. Table 9.1 lists our standard layers and their purposes.

Table 9.1   Naming scheme for layers

Layer name	Purpose
SA4A	Drafting sheet
SA4B	Space available for drawing
PART	Component profile
HIDE	Hidden detail
XHAT	Cross-hatching
CLNS	Centrelines
DIMN	Dimensions
NOTE	Annotations and text
CONS	Construction lines

For the drawing shown in Figure 9.9, the appearance of the layers might be as in Figure 9.8. It might be considered excessive to have so many layers on such a simple drawing. This is true to some extent. In practice, it is tempting to do single-layer drawings; this saves the effort of planning needed in switching from one layer to another. It is, though, useful to establish consistent working procedures from the outset and the overhead in keystrokes is not very high if drawings are layered. The result, especially when you start drawing more complicated components, is increased productivity.

AutoCAD can, in principle, have an unlimited number of layers. Each layer created will have an associated linetype and colour – for example, the layer CLNS which we have dedicated to showing centrelines will have the associated linetype CENTER. In addition, we have associated with CLNS the colour MAGENTA. This was a purely arbitrary decision and if you are working on a monochrome system, the colour attributes of layers may seem meaningless at this stage. On a colour display, though, the use of colour is a valuable aid in distinguishing different kinds of lines at comparatively low resolution. The standard AutoCAD colour set is shown in Table 9.2.

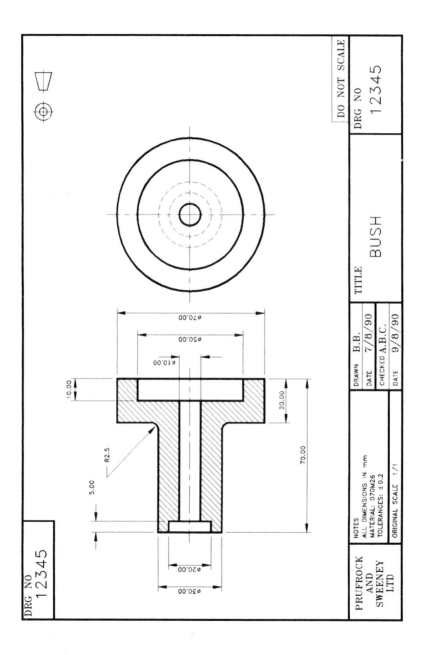

Figure 9.9 Layered drawing

Table 9.2   Standard AutoCAD colour set

Colour number	Colour Name
1	Red
2	Yellow
3	Green
4	Cyan
5	Blue
6	Magenta
7	White

We are now at a stage when we can write down our complete standard layer utilization schedule – Table 9.3.

Table 9.3   The complete layer schedule

Layer name	AutoCAD linetype	AutoCAD colour
SA4A	Continuous	White
SA4B	Continuous	Green
PART	Continuous	White
HIDE	Hidden	Blue
XHAT	Continuous	Green
CLNS	Center	Magenta
DIMN	Continuous	Green
NOTE	Continuous	Cyan
CONS	Dot	Yellow

Setting up and using layers

Since the layer schedule is to be standard, it will be incorporated into the prototype drawing A4SHEET. Later, we shall make a small amendment to give two sizes of text suitable for pen plotting.

Example. Setting up LAYERS

Brief
Set up, on the prototype drawing A4SHEET, the layer schedule shown in Table 9.3.

Plan of action
Enter AutoCAD and call up A4SHEET for editing (option 2 in the initial menu). The command sequence will include the command **LAYER** and most of its options.

Command sequence

> Command:**LAYER**
> ?/Make/Set/New/ON/OFF/Color/Ltype/Freeze/Thaw:**NEW**
> New layer name(s):**SA4A,SA4B,PART,HIDE,CLNS,XHAT,DIMN,
> NOTE,CONS**
> Linetype(or?)<CONTINUOUS>:**RETURN**
> Layer name(s) for linetype CONTINUOUS<0>:**SA4A,
> SA4B,PART,XHAT,DIMN,NOTE**
> Linetype(or?)<CONTINUOUS>:**HIDDEN**
> Layer name(s) for linetype HIDDEN<0>:**HIDE**
> Linetype(or?)<CONTINUOUS>:**CENTER**
> Layer name(s) for linetype CENTER<0>:**CLNS**
> Linetype(or?)<CONTINUOUS>:**DOT**
> Layer name(s) for linetype DOT:**CONS**

Note. The appropriate linetypes have now been allocated to the layers. Since the CONTINUOUS linetype is the default on a newly created layer, we could have omitted the command which allocated this linetype. We shall now carry on to allocate colours.

We can exit from the **LAYER** option by typing **CTRL-C** and re-enter it by typing **RETURN** at the command **Prompt**.

> Command:**RETURN**
> ?/Make/Set/New/ON/OFF/Color/Ltype/Freeze/Thaw:**C**
> Color:**GREEN**
> Layer name(s) for colour 2(Green)<0>:**HIDE, XHAT, DIMN**
>
> . . . .
> . . . .
> . . . .
> Color:**CTRL-C**
> Command:

We leave the allocation of the other colours to you. Again, there is a default on a new layer – this is WHITE. You can now check on your standard layer allocation by entering the option **LAYER** and answering the prompt with **?** and then **RETURN**. The screen will flip and you will see the full details of the allocations of both linetype and colour to each layer. There will also be a layer <0>, which is created by default when you enter the drawing editor. You can flip back to the graphics screen by hitting (probably) function key F1. If the allocation is not what is required, then the layers can be modified by again entering the **LAYER** option.

If you draw a line in one of our selected broken linetypes, you will probably find that the result is unsatisfactory. Either the gaps in the line will be of a width that is disproportionate to the size of sheet or else they will be so short that they will be difficult to see at the screen's resolution and the line will appear to be continuous. This can be remedied by setting the scale of the lines by using the command **LTSCALE**. For the moment, we shall set **LTSCALE** to the value 5. This linetype scale cannot be used selectively; it holds for all lines drawn. The command sequence is:

Command:**LTSCALE**
New scale factor <1.000>:**5**

The layer schedule is now complete and will be used for your subsequent drawings. Store it away for future use.

We have now used the commoner options in the LAYERS command. To summarize:

New   Creates a new layer
Set   Makes a layer current
ON   Makes a layer visible
OFF   Makes a layer invisible
Color   Defines the default colour of all objects drawn on a layer
Ltype   Defines the default linetype of all lines drawn on a layer
?   Displays the status of all the layers created on the drawing

Each option except **ON** and **OFF** can be called up by typing the first letter. In the case of **ON** and **OFF**, in order to avoid ambiguity, the first two letters must be used. If you do happen to only type 'O', then the system will tell you that your command is ambiguous. Of course, if you use the on-screen menu or a menu card, then there are no problems; each menu pick is unique.

The three remaining options are not so commonly used.

Make   Creates a new layer and makes it current in one operation,
Freeze Instructs AutoCAD to ignore the objects on a layer in subsequent regenerations,
Thaw   Reverses Freeze.

You can neglect these options until you are proficient with the others. Freeze and Thaw are especially useful for reducing the regeneration time in large complex drawings but it is unlikely that you will notice the difference on the modest drawings that you are probably doing now.

We shall now draw our own standard drawing sheet on the layers SA4A and SA4B that are scheduled for this purpose.

Example. **Use of layers**

Brief
Create a drawing sheet similar to the example shown in Figure 3.1 (page 25), using the layers defined in the prototype drawing.

Plan of action
Design your drawing sheet showing as a minimum all the information shown on our version in Figure 3.1. Don't forget that the primary purpose of a drawing sheet is to hold a drawing and so as little space as possible should be taken up by the frame. As we have previously mentioned, there should be a border of 15 mm minimum around the sheet. Since the size of an A4 sheet in landscape aspect ratio is 297 mm wide by 210 mm high, the outer frame of the drawing sheet should be 267 mm by 180 mm. For the moment, we shall not include any text on the frame; just concentrate

on drawing the lines (unless, of course, you have investigated the **STYLE** and **TEXT** commands). Note that, since all drafting sheets are of similar shape, the sheet can be used generally.

Command sequence
Call up the prototype drawing A4SHEET.

Turn on layers SA4A and SA4B, make SA4A current. Complete the lines on the standard drafting sheet, adding your own logo. Lines will be drawn in the linetype which has been associated with the current layer. The linetype can be altered subsequently using the **CHANGE** command, but it is best if you can keep the linetypes consistent with the layer if possible.

Next, make layer SA4B current. Draw the bounds of the space that you have left free for drafting purposes. This is not necessary, since it will not be plotted, but its use will save regeneration time. Layer SA4A can be turned **OFF** and SA4B used during the development of the drawing.

The completed sheet should look like Figure 3.1, but without the text. Save it for future use.

Exercises

1 Draw your own logo and add it to your standard drafting sheet.

2 Draw the component shown in Figure 9.9, omitting the dimensions and text for the moment. Use a systematic layer structure.

10   Annotation and hatching

A description of the standards used for lettering in engineering drawing and methods of drawing text in AutoCAD. A treatment of the principles and practice of sectioning and hatching. Commands covered are **STYLE, TEXT, DTEXT, QTEXT** and **HATCH**.

Letter fonts

Much of the information on a typical engineering component drawing is in the form of text. It is important that the lettering should be as clear as possible so that it remains readable even if the drawing is reproduced at a reduced scale. It is recommended that upper case letters should be used since the chance of misreading them at a reduced scale is lower than the chance of misreading lower case letters.

AutoCAD provides us with a wide variety of fonts useful for many applications although the more decorative are unsuitable for engineering drafting. They are grouped as follows:

Fast   Moderate quality, but drawn rapidly

Simplex   Better quality than Fast, but too thin for engineering drafting unless plotted on a multi-pen plotter with different widths of liquid ink pens

Duplex   Produced by double lines: best for display of engineering drawings

Complex   Produced by double strokes, but with serifs: too fancy for most engineering drawing applications

Triplex   Again, unsuitable for engineering drawing

Gothic   Various 'black letter' forms: unsuitable

Symbol   Sets of special non-alphanumeric symbols

Examples of each are shown in Figure 10.1. We recommend the font ROMAND (a Duplex font) for general work because it seems closest to the

```
FAST FONT TXT - TOO THIN          FAST FONT MONOTXT - TOO THIN

SIMPLEX FONT ROMANS - NOT MUCH BETTER

DUPLEX FONT ROMAND - THIS IS THE ONE WE LIKE        <=

COMPLEX FONT ROMANC - A LITTLE TOO FANCY

TRIPLEX FONT ROMANT - A LOT TOO FANCY

GOTHIC FONT GOTHICE - NOT REALLY SPACE AGE

LOTS OF OTHERS TOO - ⚕ ⚕ ♌ ♀ ⁝ · · ○ ○ ○ ◯ ◯ ◯ ▢ ▢
```

Figure 10.1 AutoCAD fonts

recommendations of BS 308. Most of the text on drawings in this book is in ROMAND. However, you should experiment to find the style which best suits your field and output devices.

The ROMAND font contains all the characters which may be found on the standard keyboard. Non-keyboard characters commonly used in drafting may be obtained by prefixing a standard keyboard character or a number which is the ASCII decimal equivalent by the escape sequence '%%'. A list of these special characters is shown below (and see Figure 10.2):

%%o	overscore
%%d	degrees symbol
%%c	diameter symbol
%%u	underscore
%%p	plus/minus symbol
%%%	percent sign

Any of the other characters in the ASCII character set may be shown by prefixing its decimal equivalent by the escape sequence; for example, %%156 will give the British pound sign.

All the AutoCAD fonts except MONOTEXT are 'proportionally spaced' to increase their visual attractiveness. Proportionally spaced characters have spaces between which are not of a constant width but vary with the characters on either side. Although this does improve the appearance of text, it makes it impossible to line text up vertically and if you have to do a lot of tabulation and wish to align characters, then you will have to use the poorer quality MONOTEXT font. If you work in an installation with a multipen plotter you may be content to use a low grade of font and use a reasonably thick pen to plot it. The ISO standard for line widths will be described later.

BS 308 does not prescribe a fixed height for lettering, but recommends the following minimum heights which are based on reprographic considerations:

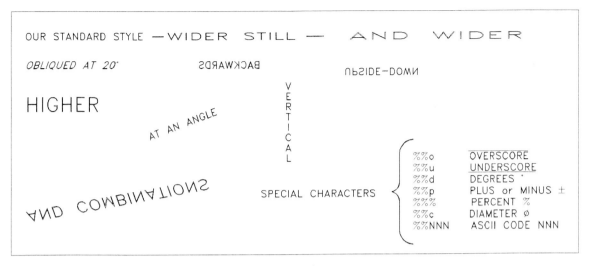

Figure 10.2 Variations in text presentation

Purpose	Sheet size	Height (mm)
Drawing numbers, etc.	A0, A1, A2, A3	7
	A4	5
Dimensions and notes	A0	3.5
	A1, A2, A3, A4	2.5

There are other, tighter standards, for example the Deutsches Institut fuer Normung (DIN) standard contains details of lettering heights and pen widths to be used with each different paper size. The ISO standard for lettering defines two styles, A and B, B being the more commonly used. The range of lettering heights is (in mm):

2.5, 3.5, 5, 7, 10, 14 and 20

The preferred line width for drawing a letter is one tenth the lettering height. It may be noticed that these are the widths and heights of the pens and lettering templates supplied by Staedtler and other firms.

The term 'font' may be defined as 'a particular geometrical configuration of a set of type'. Variants of a font are called 'styles' and, in AutoCAD, a style can be defined which is based on a font but which has its own height, width/

Table 10.1 Settings for selected standard styles

| Font name | ROMAND | ROMAND | ROMAND | ROMAND |
Style name	A0Title	A4Title	A0Notes	A4Notes
Height	7	5	3.5	2.5
Width/ht ratio	1	1	1	1
Obliquing angle	0	0	0	0
Backwards	N	N	N	N
Upside-down	N	N	N	N
Vertical	N	N	N	N

height ratio and obliquing angle. Text can also be written backwards, up-side-down and vertically, the direction of writing being considered as a quality of the style (Figure 10.2). It is best, for drafting purposes, to stick to the straightforward non-sloping (or Roman) style except for special purposes. It is occasionally useful to use directions other than left to right (for example, backwards text might be needed in the drawing of transfers). Table 10.1 shows the settings for the standard styles that we have chosen.

Note that the line width is not a property of the font style; AutoCAD leaves it to the plotter.

Creating text styles in AutoCAD

Geometric details of the standard fonts are kept in files with the extension '.SHX' – for instance, our ROMAND font is held in the file ROMAND.SHX. To create a particular style of this font, the command **STYLE** is used. To create our style A0Title, we would use the command sequence shown in the following example:

Example. Creating a text style

Brief
Create the four text styles shown in Table 10.1 and to add them to the prototype drawing.

Plan of action
Enter AutoCAD and call up A4SHEET for editing. The command sequence will include all the options in the command **STYLE**.

Command sequence
 Command:**STYLE**
 Text style name (or ?)<TEXT>:**A0TITLE**
 Font file <STANDARD>:**ROMAND**
 Height <0.00>:**7**
 Obliquing angle <0.00>:**0**
 Backwards?<Y/N>:**N**
 Upside-down?<Y/N>:**N**
 Vertical?<Y/N>:**N**
 A0TITLE is now the current text style.
 Command:

As usual with AutoCAD prompts, default settings are shown. If any of these corresponds with your desired response, you can reply with **RETURN**. The font filename should not be given an extension – '.SHX' is assumed.

 You can now carry on with the other styles in Table 10.1. When you have finished, you can check on the details of all your defined styles by responding '?' to the first prompt in **STYLE**. If there are any amendments needed, then you can redefine the styles which are in error. Now save A4SHEET for later use.

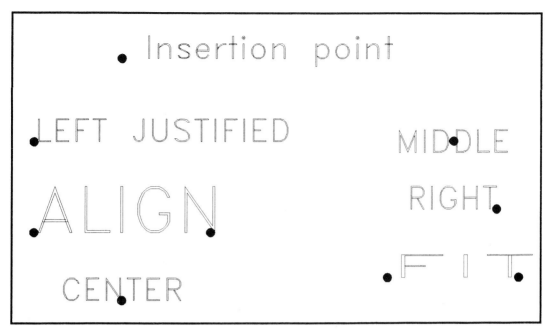

Figure 10.3   Variations in text alignment

After a text style has been created, text in that style can be placed on a drawing using the command **TEXT**, **QTEXT** or **DTEXT**. For the moment we shall only deal with **TEXT**. This command enables notes to be placed on a drawing in a given style, and at a desired position and angle. There are several options for positioning text:

Start point	This, the default, expects the operator to input the coordinates of a point which is the start position of the line of text. The text is written from the start point from left to right. This is called 'left justification'.
Align	The system asks for start and endpoints. The subsequent line of text is scaled so that it fits inside the two points.
Center	The system prompts for a point and the text is centred about that point.
Fit	Like the Align option, except that the operator must also supply a text height. The width of the text style is adjusted so that the line of text fits between the two points.
Middle	Similar to Center, except that the centre of the text is positioned at the centre of the pick rather than the middle of the bottom of the text. Text is centred both vertically and horizontally around the point returned.
Right	The line of text is positioned so that its right hand side is aligned to the input point. This is called 'right justification.'

The command **TEXT** also gives users the opportunity to change the text style, if the current style is not desired. Figure 10.3 illustrates graphically the various types of alignment. Multiple lines of text can be returned by using the **TEXT** command several times, but each time answering the prompt for start point by **RETURN** rather than by the coordinates of a point. Subsequent text may then be input and will be drawn at a fixed line spacing beneath the previous text. It will be aligned in a similar manner to the previous text drawn. However, multiple lines of text are more easily drawn using the **DTEXT** command which is described below. The command sequence for **TEXT** is:

Command:**TEXT**
Start point or Align/Center/Fit/Middle/Right/Style:**Pick option**

Since all AutoCAD text is drawn on the screen, rather than being generated by hardware as are alphanumeric characters, a drawing with a lot of annotation (for example, one with an extensive parts-list) can take a long time to regenerate. The command **QTEXT** (quick text) replaces all text by bounding rectangular boxes. This is only a temporary measure; the original text is still preserved and can be restored using the same command. **QTEXT** is a toggle, similar to **SNAP** and the command sequence is:

Command:**QTEXT**
ON/OFF<Current-setting>:**ON**
Command:

The command **DTEXT** (dynamic text) has the same alignment options as **TEXT** but allows you to return multiple lines of text. Moreover, as you return the text, it is echoed on the drawing in left-justified form. If you have chosen an alignment other than left justification, then the drawn text is adjusted after you have finished the line. For normal drawing purposes, we recommend **DTEXT** as the most convenient command.

Example. Use of DTEXT

Brief
Add the text to the standard drafting sheet held on layer SA4A on the standard prototype drawing.

Plan of action
Enter AutoCAD and call up the prototype drawing A4SHEET using option 2 on the main menu. Make layer SA4A current. Use the text styles created in the previous example to annotate the drafting sheet designed and drawn in Chapter 9.

Command sequence
Assuming that layer SA4A is current, the text is added as follows:

Command:**DTEXT**
Start point or Align/Center/Fit/Middle/Right/Style:**Style**
Style name (or ?) <CURRENT>:**A4NOTES**
Start point or Align/Center/Fit/Middle/Right/Style:**Hit start**
Height <2.5>:**RETURN**
Rotation angle <0>:**RETURN**

> Text:**DRG NUM**
> Text:**CTRL-C**
> Command:
>
> It may well be that our standard text styles do not seem to suit this application. In this case, it is best not to stick slavishly to a standard and you should select a style which pleases you. Since text is an entity, it can be erased by picking any character in the text. You can then replace it by your modified version. The finished drafting sheet should look something like Figure 3.1 (although much better!).

TEXT is one of the facilities that would have made drafters of the past very envious. Very often, drawings were judged on the quality of their printing and annotation but now all computer aided drafters can produce text of acceptable standard with little effort. There is still a lot of scope for judgement in the placement of notes so that they are clearly read. In our standard styles, we have chosen a simple form; it may be that none of the supplied fonts suit your taste. In that case, AutoCAD provides a facility for developing your own fonts. This is a long and tedious business. There are occasions when some of the more complex fonts are useful – for the letters identifying sections, a font with serifs, such as ROMANT, might be chosen. The more elaborate letter forms should be used with discretion, however, and it is best to err on the side of simplicity and to stick to fonts similar to those recommended by British and American standards.

Sections and hatching

It might be assumed that, since machining is done on the outside surface of a component, sufficient details of form could be communicated by the views and hidden lines which have been described in previous chapters. In the interests of clarity, it is often necessary to include sectional views on the drawing. On many parts there are details which are masked by the outside form. On assembly drawings it is usual for some features to be enclosed by others. It is the drafter's task to select sections in a way that will simplify the visualization of the component. There are several generally agreed conventions, used in manual drafting, which must be observed in sectional views and most of these apply to computer aided drafting.

A section is a slice through a component. This slice is taken through a cutting plane. In Figure 10.4, the part of the view where the cutting plane penetrates solid material is indicated by cross-hatching. In the early days of drafting, different materials were shown by using colour washes – for instance, cast iron was shown by Payne's grey, mild steel by Prussian blue. These drawings were beautiful to look at but must have taken a very long time to produce. As engineering production became more complex, there was a need for drawings to be reproduced. With the reprographic techniques then available (mainly blueprinting), the use of colour as an aid to communication was discontinued and different materials were shown by different hatch patterns – Figure 2.5 shows some of the patterns supplied in Auto-CAD. Nowadays, there are so many different materials that these material

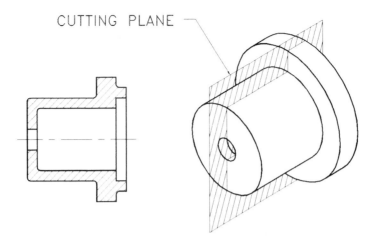

Figure 10.4   Use of crosshatching

hatch patterns are rarely used in general engineering drafting practice. Auto-CAD supplies a wide variety of hatches but we would recommend that you should restrict yourself to just one – the standard 45 degree cross-hatch pattern. Notice that this is European drafting practice; in the USA, it is common for patterns other than cross-hatching to be used.

Hatching practice

The standard AutoCAD pattern which best suits mechanical engineering drafting is ANSI31 – the American National Standard Institutes symbol for cast or malleable iron and general use. Where possible the hatchlines should be at 45 or 135 degrees from the horizontal and they should be spaced to suit the component being hatched. It is a common mistake to use a hatch with lines at too close a pitch. Not only does this result in longer regeneration times, it also causes larger drawing files. Where possible the spacing should not be less than 2.5 mm on the plot.

There are occasions when 45 degree hatching is inappropriate – Figure 10.5a shows one of these. It is wrong to use a hatch that is either parallel or perpendicular to a major part of the hatch boundary. Figure 10.5c shows another example of poor hatching practice. The two hatch islands are not aligned, even though they are both part of the same body. It is correct practice to show all the parts of one body hatched in the same pattern with interrupted hatches being aligned. In AutoCAD, each hatch pattern has a fixed datum (usually the drawing origin). If the distinct sectioned islands of a component are hatched in the same command, then all the hatches will be correctly aligned. If the islands are hatched in separate operations and the drawing origin has been changed between the operations, then the hatching may not be aligned. It is possible to use the snap grid to obtain alignment in such cases, but wherever possible you should hatch all the sectioned parts of one component in one hatch command.

Where the sections of more than two separate components abut in a view, it is necessary to use hatch angles other than 45 degrees. Since the most

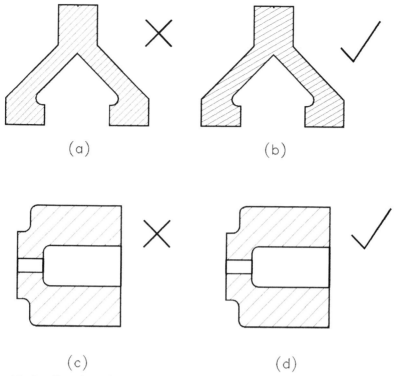

(a)   (b)

(c)   (d)

Figure 10.5   Good and bad hatching practice

complex of maps can be drawn with just four colours, it follows that the most complex of sectional views can be drawn with four hatch patterns. Again it is emphasized that clarity of communication is paramount and that you should use as many patterns as you feel are necessary to aid visualization. It is common to use not only different angles of hatch but also different hatchline spacing to distinguish separate sectioned components.

Dimensions should not normally be placed so that any part of them overlaps a hatch. On the few occasions when this is necessary, the dimension should be picked as one of the selected objects. The hatch will then be interrupted around the text.

Sectioning practice

It is usual to show a sectioned view in the position on the drawing which the unsectioned view would occupy. However, strict geometric accuracy is sometimes sacrificed in the interests of clear communication. Some of the commoner conventions are listed below.

Half sections

Symmetrical shapes are sometimes shown in half section. In Figure 10.6, notice the apparent use of the centreline as a hatch boundary line. Since it is conventional for the centreline to overlap the component profile, use of the

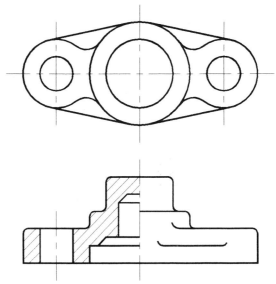

Figure 10.6 Hatching a half section

centreline in this way would very likely result in a defective hatch. The best policy in cases like this is to use a non-overlapping line for the hatch boundary, hatch the section, delete the line and then add the centreline. It may be necessary to zoom into the border of the hatch so that the boundary line can be differentiated from the hatch unless a very small aperture is set.

Broken out sections

Local sections such as that shown in Figure 9.6 (page 97) are sometimes used to save space. The irregular boundary is drawn using the **SKETCH** facility. If you try this, keep your record increment as large as possible (more on this later).

Cutting planes

Cutting planes are shown by centrelines which are thickened at their ends, with arrows indicating the direction of view. They are referred to by a pair of

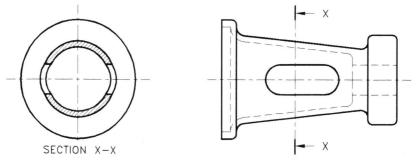

SECTION X—X

Figure 10.7 Cutting plane

letters placed close to the arrows (Figure 10.7). Polylines (to be covered in a later chapter) are particularly useful for drawing cutting planes; the centrelines can be drawn in three segments, the first and last segments being thicker than the middle one. The arrows are most conveniently drawn using the **Leader** option in **DIM**; for the moment, you will have to draw them using **LINE** with a **SOLID** arrow head. In the case of Figure 10.7, the section defined by the cutting plane would be referred to as 'Section X-X'. It is good practice to show a cutting plane, except when the position of the section is obvious – for instance if it passes through an axis of symmetry of the body.

Staggered cutting planes

It is sometimes convenient to use staggered (or 'offset') cutting planes. The cutting plane line should be drawn thicker where it changes direction (Figure 10.8). This device should not be used lightly, since the resulting drawings are often hard to read.

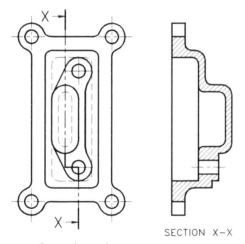

Figure 10.8 Staggered cutting plane

Ribs and thin elements

It is conventional not to section ribs and similar elements along their length (Figure 10.9). The reason for this convention should be clear if you compare Figure 10.9a with Figure 10.9b. Figure 10.9a is more geometrically correct than Figure 10.9b but it gives a completely false impression of the component. On the other hand, it *is* correct to section a rib in a transverse direction (Figure 10.9c). Where components are very thin (sheet metal parts, for example), they are usually shown by thick solid lines in section.

Bolts and similar machine elements

Bolts, shafts, rivets and like components should not be sectioned at all. The commoner machine elements have conventional representations, some of which are shown in Appendix C.

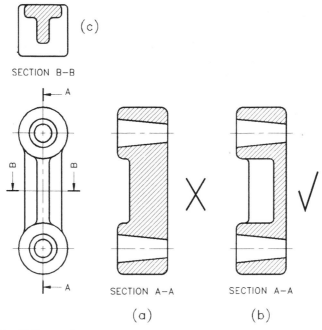

Figure 10.9   Rib section

Figure 10.10 illustrates some of the hatching principles that we have described.

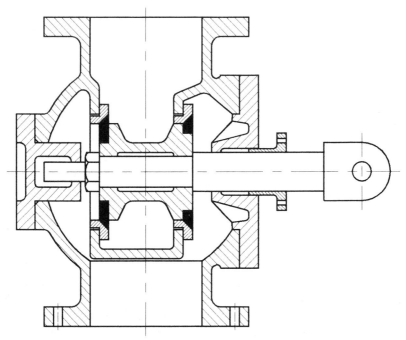

Figure 10.10   Hatching principles illustrated

Hatching in AutoCAD

In AutoCAD, we must first select the hatch pattern (ANSI31 is a good selection for general purposes, as we have previously discussed) and then define the areas to be hatched. These areas must be enclosed by precisely defined boundaries and AutoCAD, although more tolerant than some other drafting systems, is fussy about closure. Even the slightest break in a boundary, invisible on the display without zooming, may lead to a 'hatch glitch'. Possibly some of the hatchlines will be omitted or the hatch will bleed out through the gaps in the supposed boundary.

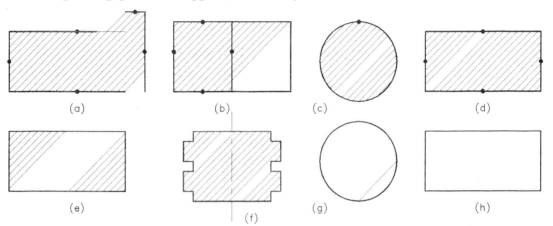

Figure 10.11   Hatching faults

Figure 10.11 shows some of the problems that might crop up. In (a) the hatch is defective because of the gaps at the top and bottom. In (b) the top and bottom lines overlap the middle vertical line to the right. Both of these cases are easily detectable on the display but the ones which follow are not so obvious. In (c) there is a small break in the circle, imperceptible at the scale of the drawing, which is just where a hatchline should hit the boundary. The same condition applies in (d) – the break is located at the bottom left corner of the rectangle. Both of these can be detected and remedied by zooming into the suspect area. In each of (a) to (d) the boundary has been selected by picking the entities which make it up; the dots show the pick points.

It is possible (and very convenient) to pick a boundary by windowing and in the next cases the boundary has been selected by this method. In these the reasons for the defective hatching cannot be detected by zooming. In (e), the top and bottom lines of the rectangle have been duplicated, with the overlaid lines defined in opposite directions. If either the top or bottom line is picked then only one of the overlapping lines will be added to the selection set. However, if windowing is used, then all the entities lying within the window will be selected and both sets of overlapping lines will be added to the selection set. The only way to detect this easily is to check the number of entities that the system reports it has found. In the case of (e) the number will be six instead of the expected four. As we have mentioned before, it is beneficial to get into the habit of checking the system responses after a command has been executed.

The reason for hatch failure in case (f) would be undetectable even if the user were alert enough to check on the number of entities found. The symmetrical section has been formed by mirroring about the vertical centreline but the top and bottom horizontal lines of the half section are not flush to the centreline; they pass it by a small amount. The result is that the mirrored form has overlaps at top and bottom. This is difficult to detect since the display will look correct even if it is zoomed and the windowing operation will report the expected number of found entities. Extreme cases of hatch defects are shown in (g) and (h) which are admittedly artificial. In (g) the circle is made up of four arcs, overlapping in pairs. One pair make up a circle, the other pair do not quite make up a circle and are defined in the opposite sense to the first pair. In (h) there are two rectangles defined in opposite directions. In the last case, probably the most pathological, the system has produced no error messages and considers that the hatching is a job well done. But no hatchlines have been produced at all.

Inclusion of these cases is not intended as a criticism of AutoCAD which is better than many larger and more expensive systems in its toleration of defective boundaries. It must be appreciated that hatching, like other computer aided drafting facilities, is performed by a deterministic procedure which requires exactly defined parameters. It might be feasible for a superintelligent hatching procedure to make an assumption about the user's intention; this assumption might, of course, be incorrect. It is probably better for decisions to be left to the user than to allow the system to improvise, since this results in a more flexible system. Hatching is a typical case where *Previous Planning Prevents Poor Performance*. Remedying deficiencies in hatch boundaries is often not straightforward and it is best to bear hatching in mind when the section is drawn.

A technique, useful when difficulties occur with hatching, is to overdraw the hatch boundary using a polyline on the hatch layer. If separate closed polylines are used for each hatch island, and lines drawn on the hatch layer have a different colour from those used for the outline of the part (as on our standard prototype drawing), then there should be no problem in achieving an acceptable hatch. Some other tactics will be discussed later in this section.

A command sequence for hatching is:

Command:**HATCH**
Pattern(? or name/U,style) < default pattern > :**ANSI31**
Scale for pattern < default scale > :**20**
Angle for pattern < default angle > :**0**
Select objects:**Now pick the hatch boundary**

As usual, if we reply to a prompt by **RETURN**, then the default is assumed. **?** gives a listing of all available standard patterns. **U** allows the user to define a simple crosshatch pattern. If this is selected, the system returns:

Angle for crosshatch lines < default > :
Spacing between lines < default > :
Double hatch area? < default > :

The angle and spacing may be chosen to suit the application. If **N** is answered to the question, then the conventional single hatch will be generated; if **Y** is returned, then a second pattern will be drawn over the first, but at 90 degrees to it. Since, as we have discussed, crosshatching is the preferred pattern in engineering drawing, you may choose to use the **U** option exclusively.

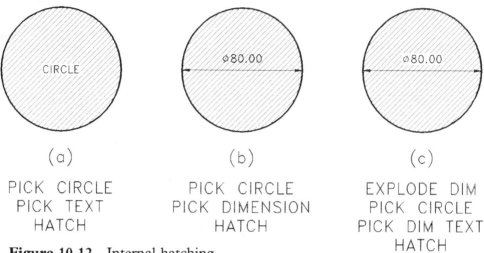

PICK CIRCLE   PICK CIRCLE   EXPLODE DIM
PICK TEXT   PICK DIMENSION   PICK CIRCLE
HATCH   HATCH   PICK DIM TEXT
                                         HATCH

Figure 10.12   Internal hatching

Boundaries are usually simple in engineering drawing – the connected chain of entities does not normally enclose any other items (except, possibly, text). If there are any items inside the outer boundary and they are not selected, then they will be hatched over, just as if they did not exist. If internal items are selected, then hatching may be done in one of three ways – Normal (N), Outermost (O) or Ignore (I) – see Figure 10.12. Any of these styles may be selected by following the style name by 'N','O' or 'I', for example, 'ANSI31,I'. Although using these three hatch styles might save the odd key stroke, it is recommended that you select entities individually, even if your boundary does enclose other boundaries and text.

Example. **Hatching**

Brief
Hatch the view shown in Figure 10.13.

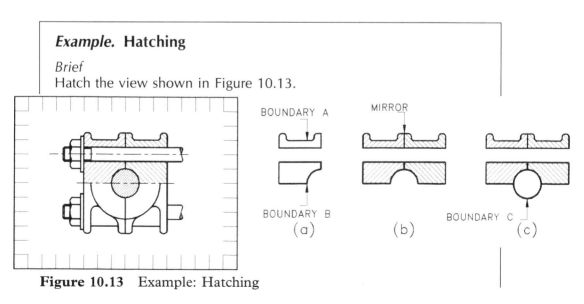

Figure 10.13   Example: Hatching

Plan of action
The UCS is placed at the centre of the hole in the middle. The section contains five hatching islands. Do them first so that the hatch boundaries can be checked easily. They are most conveniently done by drawing the left pair of islands first (Figure 10.13a). Since they are both part of a single component, they must be hatched using the same hatch pattern and with each section of hatch aligned. Both of these conditions can be observed if they are hatched with one command.

Also, since the part is symmetrical, the hatch on the left side can be mirrored to give the different hatch pattern needed on the right. The circle can be added separately. There should be no problem in picking the circle as a boundary since it is partially remote from boundaries A and B. Where there are separate boundaries sharing the same lines or arcs, AutoCAD usually selects the most recently defined when the super-imposed objects are picked.

Command sequence
Draw the left two islands (Figure 10.13a) and hatch them using the sequence:

> Command:**HATCH**
> Pattern(? or name/U,style)<default>:**ANSI31**
> Scale for pattern<default>:**20**
> Angle for pattern:**0**
> Select objects:**Pick boundaries A and B**

Since the boundaries are disjoint, there should be no difficulty in hatching them. If you have defined the forms with line and arc entities, then you can pick them individually or by a selection window.

Mirror them about the centreline (Figure 10.13b) by:

> Command:**MIRROR**
> Select objects:**W**
> First corner:**Pick a corner of the window box**
> Second corner:**Pick the other corner**
> Select objects:**RETURN**
> First point of mirror line:**0,0**
> Second point:**0,10**

The circle in the centre should now be hatched (Figure 10.13c). This is left for you to do.

The hatching should now be complete. Finish off the drawing.

Notes
There are several techniques that can be used in hatching complex boundaries:

- The boundaries can be defined as sets of completely separate entities.
- The hatches can be done remotely from the main view and assembled like a jigsaw puzzle.
- The hatch boundaries can be defined as a set of separate polylines. This was the technique used above. It gives good results on the screen

or on an electrostatic plotter but some of the lines overlap, which might give unsatisfactory results on a pen plotter.

- If speed is essential and a bad hatch has occurred, then you can explode the hatch block and edit or add individual hatchlines manually. This is not good practice but is probably the fastest way (and no one need ever know). Note that one of the hatchlines on Figure 10.13 had to be added after the **HATCH** command had given a bad hatch because of a bad line definition. Can you tell which?

Exercises

1   Annotate some of the drawings that you have done earlier. Use **DTEXT**.

2   Reproduce the drawing shown in Figure 10.10 paying special attention to good hatching practice.

3   Draw some of the hatched figures in Figure 10.14.

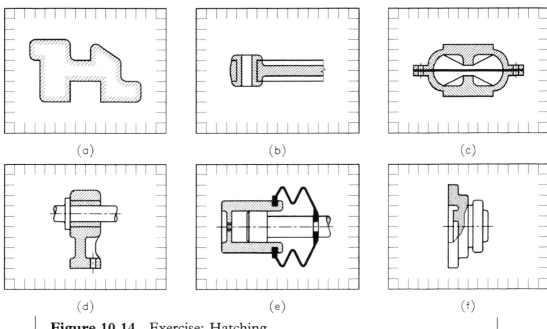

(a)   (b)   (c)

(d)   (e)   (f)

Figure 10.14   Exercise: Hatching

11 Dimensions and tolerances

An introduction to dimensioning and tolerancing practice. The **DIM** and **DIM1** commands are dealt with in detail.

Introduction to dimensioning

The engineering detail drawing is the most informative record of a component; an essential part of the drawing is the dimensioning. Dimensions are used to position features, to size features and to provide details of gauging. The drafter has to make sure that the drawing is correct but also, since the interpreters of drawings are usually working from prints sometimes reduced in scale and often in a dirty environment, it is of extreme importance that dimensions should be as clear as possible. If a part has been drawn to scale on a computer aided drafting system then its dimensions are defined exactly, but this is not enough. The dimensions should be shown so that they are readable by a human being with no possibility of misunderstanding.

The shape of a component can be defined by a variety of dimensioning arrangements. Even a form as simple as that shown in Figure 11.1a can be defined by many sets of dimensions, some of which are shown in Figures 11.1b to 11.1e.

Each of these dimensioning systems satisfies two basic rules of dimensioning practice:

- Dimensioning systems should be *complete* – it should be possible to redraw the form exactly from the dimensions given.
- Dimensioning systems should be *minimal* – no redundant dimensions should be present.

Occasionally, these rules are not observed in practice. In casting drawings, parts of a form are sometimes left to the discretion of the patternmaker –

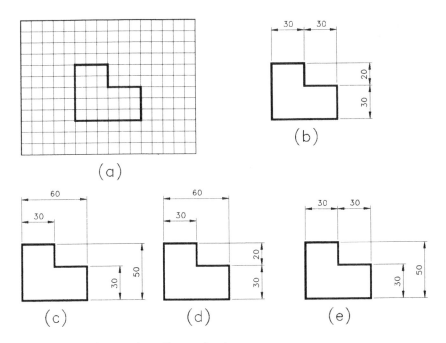

Figure 11.1 Alternative dimensioning systems

these parts are usually cosmetic, however. They are invariably drawn attention to by some note such as 'Blend to suit'. And sometimes redundant dimensions are included for the convenience of the inspector. These 'auxiliary' dimensions are always indicated by a note such as 'reference only' or by being enclosed in parentheses.

In practice, for a given component, one of the possible dimensioning systems will be more suitable than the others.

This will be discussed in further sections. In the absence of any other information, it is considered good practice to dimension features from common reference edges or datums. In Figure 11.2, for example, all features are dimensioned from the two datum faces AF and AB. It is regarded also as bad practice to dimension from a datum which is outside the part being dimensioned, except in very special circumstances.

Dimensioning – linear dimensions

Commonly, the extents of dimension lines are shown by arrowheads (Figures 11.1b – 11.1e). Although this is the most usual method, there are others – ticks and dots are sometimes used (Figure 11.3). We shall use the form prescribed by BS 308 and similar widely used standards (Figure 11.4). Some other features of standard dimensioning practice are:

- Dimension and witness (or 'projection' or 'extension') lines should be thinner than the lines used for the outline of the part. ISO standard line widths are listed in Chapter 9.
- It is usual to leave a small gap between the feature being dimensioned and

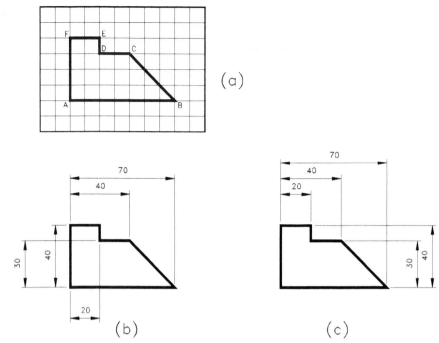

Figure 11.2 Reference datums

the start of the witness line and to extend the witness line by a small amount beyond the dimension line.

- Dimension text is shown near the middle of, and clear of, the dimension line.
- On horizontal dimensions, the text should be above the dimension lines: on vertical dimensions, the text should be to the left of dimension lines.
- Dimensions should be readable from the bottom and right of the drawing.
- Dimensions should be placed on the view which shows the relevant feature in its most characteristic form and, if possible, outside the profile of the component.
- If a feature is not to scale, attention should be drawn to it by underlining the appropriate dimensions. This practice is common in manual drafting where drawings are often modified dimensionally without changing the

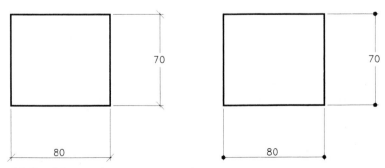

Figure 11.3 Alternative representations

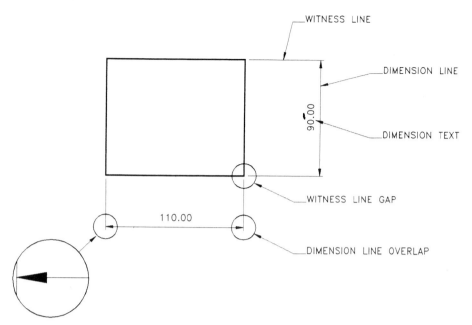

Figure 11.4 Standard dimension presentation

shape of the component. It is a practice not to be recommended and should not be necessary when a computer aided drafting system is being used.

• Suggested minimum heights for dimension text are 3.5 mm for A0 sheets and 2.5 mm for A1, A2, A3 and A4 sheets.

These practices are not universal. In the US, for example, dimension text is often placed horizontally regardless of the angle of the dimension line. And text is often written so that it cuts the dimension line. AutoCAD allows users to customize the dimensioning system to cater for local variations of standard and usage.

Linear dimensioning in AutoCAD

In AutoCAD, the form of dimensions is much more flexible than in many other drafting systems and can be tailored to suit the user's preferences or installation standards. Dimensioning is performed by using the commands: **DIM** or **DIM1**. The difference between these commands is that **DIM** is a complete and complex sub-system, suitable if many dimensions are to be added to a drawing; **DIM1** is handy for adding just one isolated dimension to a drawing. Drafting procedures vary from person to person, but it is a widespread practice to complete all the views of the component and then add all the dimensions in one process. This method is well-suited by **DIM**. Alternatively, when drawing modification is being done, it is common for just one or two dimensions to be added. This is a job for **DIM1**.

Users can control the way in which dimensions are shown by adjusting a wide variety of dimension variables (**Dim Vars**). A full list of these variables is given in Appendix B. While drawing, the user can examine the current settings of the variables by using the command sequence **DIM STATUS**. Any of the variables can be set by the command **DIM** followed by the **Dim Var** name. Some of the variables are set to numeric values – **DIMTXT** is the height of the dimension text, **DIMTVP** is the gap between text and dimension line in units of the text height. Others are flags which are set to **ON** or **OFF** – **DIMTAD** forces the text to be above the dimension line rather than through it.

Table 11.1   Dimension variable settings

Dim Var	Setting	Description
DIMEXO	2	Witness line gap
DIMEXE	2	Witness line overlap
DIMASZ	4	Arrowhead length
DIMTXT	3.5	Dimension text height
DIMTAD	ON	Text above dimension line
DIMTIH	OFF	Text horizontal and inside dimension line
DIMTOH	OFF	Text outside dimension line
DIMTSZ	0	Tick size
DIMTVP	1	Gap between text and dimension line

A suggested setting for general engineering use is shown in Table 11.1. These settings give reasonable results; they may need to be re-set temporarily during the course of drawing. You will find it useful to add them to your standard prototype drawing A4SHEET. You should enter AutoCAD and call up drawing A4SHEET for editing (Option 2 in the Main Menu). Each variable should then be set as follows:

Command:**DIM**
Dim:**DIMEXO**
Current value <2.50> New value:**2**
Dim:**DIMEXE**

. . . .
. . . .
Dim:**EXIT**

Example. Use of horizontal and vertical dimensions

Brief
Dimension, in accordance with good practice, the form shown in Figure 11.2a (page 124).

Plan of action
Select datum edges AB and AF. Place dimensions above and to the right so that projection lines cross material as little as possible.

Command sequence
Draw the component. Since all dimensions are multiples of 10 drawing units, use a snap grid. Then add the dimensions, first the horizontal, then the vertical:

> Command:**DIM**
> Dim:**Horizontal**
> First extension line origin or RETURN to select:**Pick F**
> Second extension line origin:**Pick E**
> Dimension line location:**Pick suitable point**
> Dimension text<20.00>:**20**
> Dim:**RETURN**
> Horizontal
> First extension line origin or RETURN to select:**Pick F**
> Second extension line origin:**Pick C**
>
> . . . .

Carry on with the remaining horizontal dimensions. Now do the vertical dimensions:

> Dim:**Vertical**
> First extension line origin or RETURN to select:**Pick B**
> Second extension line origin:**Pick C**
>
> . . . .

Carry on with the other vertical dimensions. When all dimensions are done, exit the **DIM** sub-system:

> Dim:**EXIT**

Notes
Figures 11.2b and 11.2c show two results of the procedure given above. Which is the better and why? This illustrates that even when using a drafting system, it is important to remember that you are attempting to create an effective piece of engineering communication.

The system response to the commands **Horizontal** and **Vertical** was:

> First extension line origin or RETURN to select:

In the case above we picked the points where the extension line intersected the feature to be dimensioned and were then prompted for the second point. If we had replied with **RETURN** to the first prompt, then we could have pointed directly to an entity and the system would have automatically worked out the extension line origins for us. This is not a very useful option and you are advised to forget it and pick extension line origins explicitly.

The system gives users the opportunity to insert their own dimension text. In the example, the system told us that the measured dimension text by default was '20.00'. We preferred to insert '20'. The number of decimal places may be adjusted by the command **UNITS**, which we have already met.

The sub-commands **Horizontal** and **Vertical** force the dimension lines (if possible) to the angles 0 and 90 degrees regardless of the relative positions of the pick points. There are two other options which also force the dimension line to a desired angle: **Aligned** and **Rotated**. **Aligned** results in the dimension line lying parallel with the line joining the two pick points; **Rotated** forces the dimension line to lie at an arbitrary angle which is input by the user. Their actions are illustrated in Figures 11.5a–d.

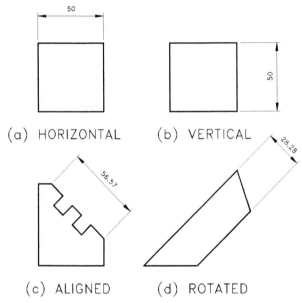

(a) HORIZONTAL (b) VERTICAL

(c) ALIGNED (d) ROTATED

Figure 11.5 Direction of dimension lines

Often, dimensions occur in associated groups. Two cases are catered for in AutoCAD: **Baseline** and **Continued**. The most useful is **Baseline** which permits the user to dimension a group of features from a common datum point. The first pick point of the first dimension is assumed automatically to be the first pick point of subsequent dimensions. Each dimension is offset from the previous one by a fixed amount, the magnitude offset being adjustable by setting a dimension variable **DIMDLI**. The dimensions in Figure 11.6a could have been drawn by the command sequence:

Command:**DIM**
Dim:**DIMDLI**
Current value <5.00>:**10**
Dim:**Horizontal**
First extension line origin or RETURN to select:**Pick A**
Second extension line origin:**Pick B**
Dimension line location:**Pick C**
Dimension text <30.00>:**30**
Dim:**Baseline**
Second extension line origin:**Pick D**
Dimension text <60.00>:**60**
Dim:**RETURN**

Second extension line origin:**Pick E**
Dimension text < 100.00 >:**100**

. . . .

Similarly with the vertical dimensions and then:

Dim:**Exit**
Command:

Rather more rarely used is the command **Continued**. Each dimension, instead of being offset, is placed in line with the previous one. Figure 11.6b shows its action, the command sequence being similar to that of **Baseline**

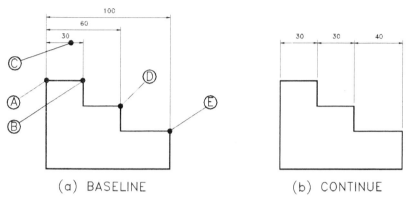

(a) BASELINE   (b) CONTINUE

Figure 11.6   Grouped dimensions

except that **DIMDLI** need not be set. This type of dimension results in a cumulative build-up of permitted tolerance between the first and last points, which is often undesirable.

Standards for circular and angular dimensions

Diametral dimensions are used for circular features – cylinders and holes. It is normally considered bad practice to dimension circular features by quoting radii because generally gauging tools use diametral measurement. Dimensioning of circles is often one of the less satisfactory features of computer aided drafting. It is worth spending some time experimenting with the commands available in AutoCAD until an adequate standard can be attained.

It has previously been stated that the view chosen for dimensioning should be the most characteristic view of a feature. In the interests of clarity, this principle is commonly ignored for cylindrical components. Where there is a possibility of confusing the dimensions of a set of concentric circles, drawing standards are unanimous in recommending that dimensions be placed on side views (Figure 11.7). It should be noted that the standard European practice is to precede diametral dimensions by the character 'ϕ' (you may remember that in AutoCAD text this is a special character '%%C'). This is obviously useful in cases such as Figure 11.7. If it is made clear that dimensions are diametral, then the end view is strictly redundant; although it is

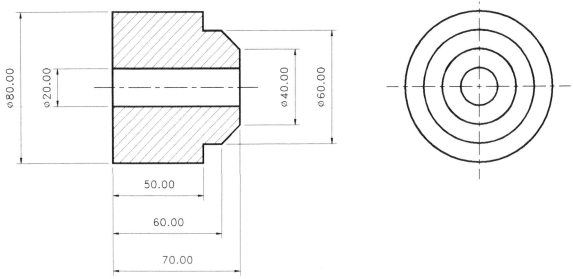

Figure 11.7 Dimensions of concentric circles

usually added to aid visualization. There are other standards: in the USA (and occasionally elsewhere), the abbreviation 'DIA' is used; often, if it is obvious from the form of the component that the dimension is diametral, then nothing apart from the dimension is quoted. We would support BS 308's recommendation, that all diametral dimensions be preceded by 'ϕ'.

Again, the principle of dimensioning the most characteristic view is sometimes ignored by using leader lines instead of dimension lines on side views of cylindrical objects. This device is especially useful for components such as stepped shafts (Figure 11.8).

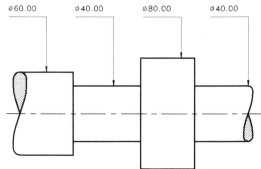

Figure 11.8 Dimensions indicated by leader lines

For simple circular forms, the four dimensioning systems shown in Figure 11.9 are used. These are primarily suitable for the following applications:

(a) for cylindrical objects
(b) for holes
(c) for small cylindrical objects
(d) for small holes

but can be used generally if it helps to make the dimensioning clear.

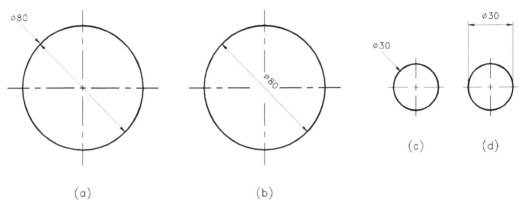

Figure 11.9 Dimensioning simple circular forms

Structural members often have many holes and dimensioning their positions and sizes by conventional means can lead to a confusing drawing. It is common practice to allocate letters to holes and groups of holes and to show their sizes by a hole schedule (Figure 11.10). Sometimes, not only are the hole diameters quoted this way but also the coordinates of the hole centres. This is a typical practice in the detailing of automobile structural members.

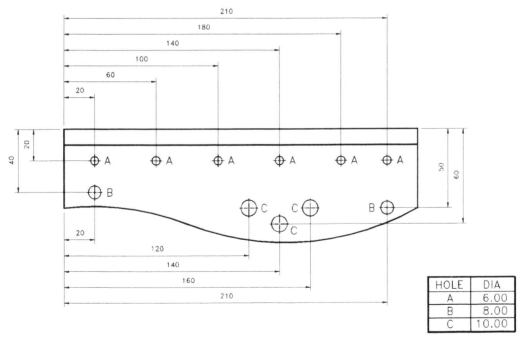

Figure 11.10 Hole schedule for multiple holes

Small holes are usually dimensioned not by dimension line and text but by using a descriptive note with a leader line. Not only does the note contain details of the hole diameters but also features such as 'through' and 'countersink'.

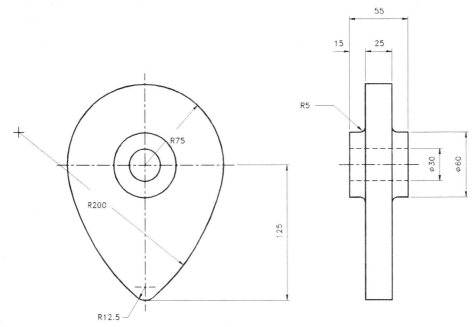

Figure 11.11   Radial dimensioning

Figure 11.11 shows some examples of radial dimensioning. Two points to notice are that radii are preceded by the letter 'R' and that the dimension line is a leader line which is in line with the centre of the arc being dimensioned. The preferred angle of radial dimension lines is 45 degrees; of course, this can be waived if the result is a clearer drawing.

Spherical features are dimensioned radially and their radii are preceded by 'SPHERE R'.

Examples of angular dimensioning are shown in Figure 11.12. The angle between two lines is shown by witness lines extended from the lines; the dimension line is an arc with centre at the intersection of the lines. Where possible the dimensions should be placed in the angular gap rather than on material (as in Figure 11.12c) even if this involves reentrant angles. The angle of the text is sometimes a difficulty in angular dimensioning. If in doubt use horizontal dimension text. It is standard engineering drawing practice to dimension angles in degrees and minutes.

There are very few rules which apply to the use of leader lines. Figure 11.13 shows some points of good practice. Note that where a leader line points to a line it should make an angle with the line as close as possible to 90 degrees and that leader lines should not intersect. It is a common practice on assembly drawings to terminate the leader lines pointing to components not with arrows but with dots.

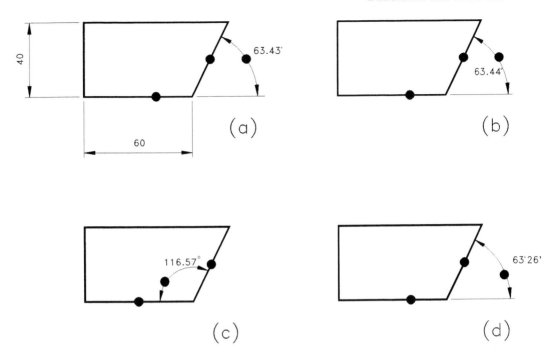

Figure 11.12 Angular dimensioning

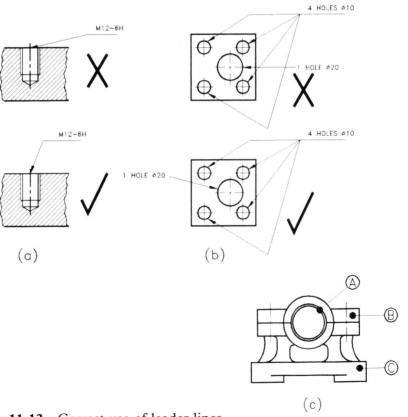

Figure 11.13 Correct use of leader lines

Circular and angular dimensions in AutoCAD

There is only one circular dimensioning command in AutoCAD. This is **Diameter**, a sub-command of **DIM**. The command sequence is:

Command:**DIM**
Dim:**Diameter**
Select arc or circle:**Pick the circle to be dimensioned**
Dimension text<Measured diameter>:**RETURN or TEXT**

Again, if you input **RETURN**, then the default measured diameter text is used. The action is similar to that of linear dimensioning except that the text is preceded by the character 'ϕ'. Other options are to type the text that you wish to replace the default text or to type a space which will result in no text at all being written.

The major difference between linear and circular dimensioning is that successful circular dimensioning requires more judgement. When the circle for dimensioning is selected, the position of the pick point governs the position of the diametral dimension line. The dimension line passes through the centre of the circle and the pick point on its circumference. It is usual to pick the circle away from its quadrant points so that there is little possibility of the dimension line being confused with the centrelines; it may be remembered that we earlier stated a rule that centrelines should not be used as dimension lines. Where circles are dimensioned internally, it is probably best to depart from standard practice and use small centre marks rather than the normal centrelines overlapping the diameter. The **Diameter** command can provide centre marks automatically, the dimension variable **Dimcen** being set to the size of centre mark required.

One technique to improve circular dimensioning is to suppress dimension text altogether during the **Diameter** command and write it in later at a position away from the centre of the circle. Another method is to dimension the circle, then **EXPLODE** the dimension and adjust the text using the **MOVE** command. This probably leads to the best results and is satisfactory for a small number of circles. If it is necessary to dimension many, it becomes rather tedious.

Another complication in circular dimensioning is that the form of dimensioning is conditioned by the relative sizes of the dimension text, the arrowhead and the circle being dimensioned. There are three cases:

- The text, the dimension line and the arrowheads fit inside the circle (Figure 11.9b). The circle is dimensioned normally.
- The dimension line and arrowheads fit inside the circle but the text does not (Figure 11.9a). AutoCAD responds:

Text does not fit. Enter leader length for text.

You can then pick the end of a leader line which is constructed in line with the pick point and the circle centre and outside the circle. The text is placed at the end of the leader line. In order to aid selection of a suitable location for the text, the end of the leader line is rubberbanded to the pick point. If you answer the request for a length by **RETURN**, then AutoCAD automatically provides a small leader line. If the angle of the leader line is greater than 15 degrees from horizontal, then a short, horizontal extension to the leader is also drawn.

- If dimension line, arrowheads and text do not fit inside the circle, then the dimension text is placed outside the circle with a leader line pointing to the circle (Figure 11.9c).

The uncertainty of the results of dimensioning using **Diameter** provide a high degree of motivation for taking the advice given previously, that cylindrical objects should be dimensioned not on the view showing the circular end, but on the side view. This can be done by using linear dimensions and replacing the measured text by the desired value prefixed by '%%C' (Figure 11.9d).

Leader lines are drawn by selecting the option **Leader**. This option is easy to use, the only point to bear in mind is that the start point is the end of the leader line with the arrow. The leader line can then be drawn, if necessary in a continuous series of line segments. On completion of the leader line, the command prompts for the text to be inserted. It automatically adds a short line segment to the text if you want text to be added automatically. If not, you can prematurely exit from the leader line option by using **CTRL-C**. This does not quit the **DIM** sub-system. In this case, the text can be added subsequently using the normal **TEXT** command.

Angular dimensions work much like linear dimensions except that four, instead of three, pick points are provided. The sub-command **Angular** works as follows:

Command:**Angular**
Select first line:**Pick a line**
Second line:**Pick a line**
Enter dimension arc location:**Pick a point**
Dimension text <measured angle>:**RETURN for measured text** or **Your own text** or **SPACE** for no text.
Enter text location:**Pick point for start of text**

It is unnecessary for the lines to intersect. The angle selected is always less than 180 degrees. The text that you type can be followed by '%%d' – the conventional degree sign. Examples of angular dimensioning are shown in Figure 11.12 on which the dots represent the pick points. Note that the appearance of the angular dimension depends on the point picked to locate the dimension arc; either of the angles less than, or greater than, 90 degrees can be generated.

Radial dimensions may be drawn by using the option **Radius**. The action of this option is similar to that of the leader line option. Examples are shown in Figure 11.11.

Introduction to tolerancing theory

Up to now we have been dimensioning parts as though all their features were of precise size. In practice, the size of a feature can only be guaranteed to be

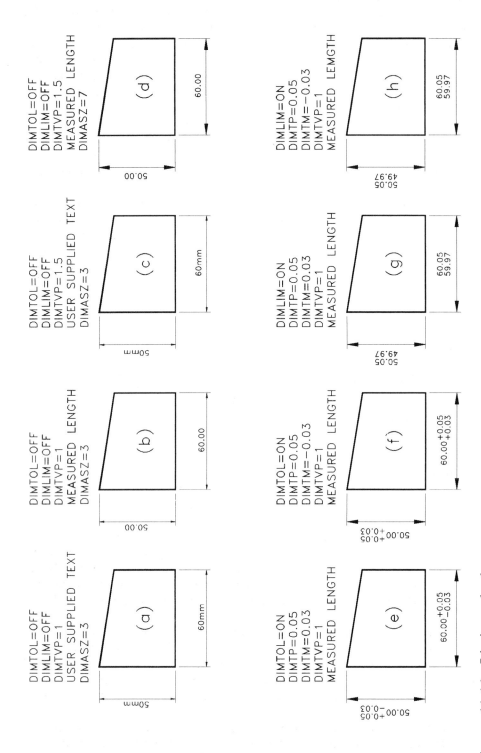

Figure 11.14 Limits and tolerances

within limits which depend on the process used to make it. The area of uncertainty is called 'tolerance'. The tolerances on the dimensions of a component must be specified by the designer in such a way that the component can fulfil its function satisfactorily. Since high precision involves high cost, it is also a requirement that the tolerances should be as wide as possible without adversely affecting function. Because of this compromise between functional requirement and manufacturing cost, the selection of tolerance is a complicated business.

Besides size, there are other functional requirements which often have to be specified by the designer; these include material selection, surface texture and hardness. Again, these require a detailed technical knowledge.

It is a recommendation of BS 308 that component drawings should primarily show the tolerances which are essential for the satisfactory functioning of the component and that production processes and inspection methods should not be shown except on drawings which are specifically intended for those purposes. Despite this, it is necessary that appropriate production methods should be borne in mind during tolerance selection so that realistic tolerances are quoted. Similarly, it is the responsibility of the production planner to choose processes which give tolerances at least as fine as those specified by the designer.

Tolerancing practice

There are two main methods of defining limits on a dimension.

Maximum/minimum limits (Figure 11.14g and h).
Bilateral tolerances (Figure 11.14e and f).

The maximum/minimum system quotes the actual extreme values between which the dimension can lie. In the bilateral tolerance method, a nominal dimension is quoted with the two deviations from it. These are usually, but by no means always, plus and minus values. An example of a case in which two positive deviations might be used is on a shaft which is a drive fit in a cylinder.

It is standard practice to use the same number of decimal places for both upper and lower limits in the maximum/minimum system. Similarly, in the bilateral tolerance system, both tolerances are quoted to the same number of decimal places; the nominal size, however, can be quoted to fewer decimal places. An exception to this rule is that if one of the tolerances is zero, then it is usual just to write '0'.

Tolerances are either specified directly on dimensions or defined by some general note such as 'unspecified tolerances ± 0.1'. It is unusual to see a part fully toleranced – non-critical dimensions are often quoted at nominal values and there are almost always neglected tolerances such as squareness.

Angular tolerances should be expressed, like angles, in degrees, minutes and, possibly, seconds.

A common functional requirement is that two components should fit together in some defined way – for instance, it might be required that one should slide on the other or that they should fit tightly enough to provide a fixed joint under load. These conditions are often described informally by terms such as 'loose running', 'light press' and 'transition'. There are national standards such as BS 4500 'ISO limits and fits' and ANSI 'Preferred limits and fits for cylindrical parts' which enumerate the tolerances needed to result in functional relations between parts. Tolerances on shaft and hole are given standard codes such as 'e8' and 'H7', and these codes are often quoted instead of the explicit tolerances.

There are also standards for specifying surface textures – ISO/R 1302 'Method of indicating surface texture on drawings' is one.

The commoner machine components such as screw threads, keyways, splines and tapers each have preferred methods for dimensioning which are defined in national standards, and are often governed by practical consideration of gauging methods.

It is the detail designer's responsibility to be familiar with these standards and to use the dimensional systems recommended in them. A skilled detail designer should, ideally, have a knowledge of the functional specification of a component, should be familiar with the processes that will produce it and should be aware of the gauging methods which will be used to check that it complies with the drawing. In many cases, detail design is assisted by consultation with specialists in a firm.

The variation of form or position of a feature is called its 'geometric tolerance'. There is a set of widely used ISO standard symbols for geometric tolerance which are shown in Appendix A. Each symbol defines a tolerance zone within which the relevant feature must lie. Tolerance symbols are used with tolerance frames which show the type of tolerance zone, the magnitude of the tolerance and the datum to which they apply. BS 308 recommends standard proportions for tolerance frames and firms often impose their use as standard. On computer aided drafting systems, it is usual to define tolerance frames as standard pre-defined blocks which users can add to drawings without having to draw them. Blocks are discussed in Chapter 13.

It should be clear by now that selecting tolerances is a complex and critical activity. We shall not deal with the *selection* of tolerances, merely with the means for their *specification*.

Tolerances in AutoCAD

Both bilateral tolerances and maximum/minimum limits can be added to dimension text conveniently in AutoCAD. The tolerance style used is determined by the setting of two dimension variables flags: **DIMTOL** and **DIMLIM**.

- If both **DIMTOL** and **DIMLIM** are **OFF**, no tolerances at all will be added to dimensions. This condition has been in force for the dimensioning that we have been doing up to now.
- If **DIMTOL** is **ON** (which forces **DIMLIM** to **OFF**), then the system will add bilateral tolerances to subsequent dimension text.
- If **DIMLIM** is **ON** (which forces **DIMTOL** to **OFF**), then the system will replace the usual dimension text by maximum/minimum limits.

Procedures for adding tolerances

Preparation
Set the number of decimal places (if different from the current setting) by using the command **UNITS**.

Bilateral tolerances
1 In **DIM**, set the dimension variable **DIMTOL ON**.
2 Set dimension variable **DIMTP** to the plus tolerance.
3 Set dimension variable **DIMTM** to the minus tolerance.
4 Dimension the entity required. Since the lower tolerance is obtained by negating the value in **DIMTM**, plus/plus tolerances can be produced by entering a negative number for **DIMTM**.

Maximum/minimum limits
1 In **DIM**, set the dimension variable **DIMLIM ON**.
2 Set dimension variable **DIMTP** to the upper tolerance.
3 Set dimension variable **DIMTM** to the lower tolerance.
4 Dimension the entity required. The upper limit is obtained by adding the value in **DIMTM** to the nominal dimension found by the system. The lower limit is obtained by subtracting the value in **DIMTP** from the nominal dimension found by the system.

Associative dimensioning

In computer aided drafting, 'associative dimensioning' means that a dimension is tied logically to the entity that it references in such a way that if the entity changes size then so also will the dimension. In non-associative dimensioning, the dimension has no logical connection with the entity, they are completely independent and a change in the size of the entity will have no effect on the dimensioning. Clearly, associative dimensioning is the more immediately useful in normal circumstances. An entity can be scaled or stretched and the operator need not re-dimension it. In AutoCAD, dimensioning is associative only if the dimension variable **DIMASO** is switched **ON**.

A dimension consists of dimension lines, extension lines, arrowheads and dimension text. If associative dimensioning is in force, then all these are treated as one entity. If **DIMASO** is switched **OFF**, then each element of the dimension is a separate entity and can be edited individually – for example, dimension text can be moved relative to the dimension line. You have probably been working with associative dimensions already, since the default setting of **DIMASO** is **ON**.

If an object is associatively dimensioned, then it uses definition points which are kept automatically on a special layer called **DEFPOINTS**. These definition points compactly define the positions of the various elements of the dimensioning system – for instance, a linear dimension is defined by just three points. If you want to see these definition points, then you can turn the

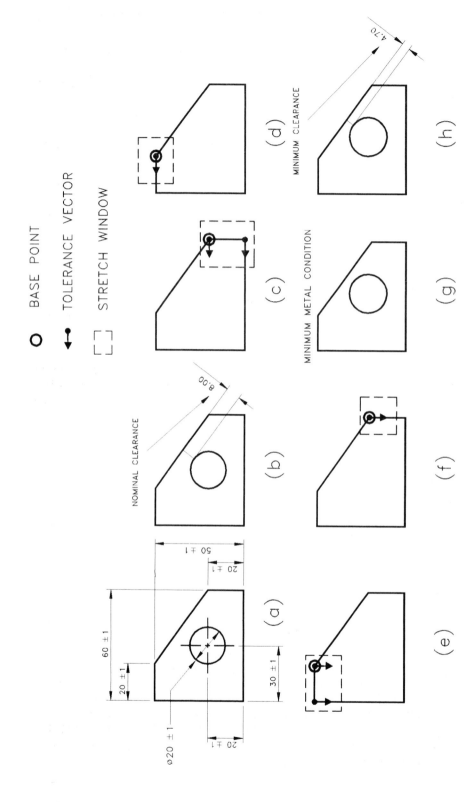

Figure 11.15 Use of STRETCH in tolerancing

DEFPOINTS layer **ON**. The definition points for the various dimensioning systems are:

- Linear dimensions: the points used to specify the extension lines and the point where the dimension line intersects the first extension line.
- Diametral dimensions: the point used to select the circle and the point diametrically opposite to it.
- Radial dimensions: the point used to select the arc and the centre point of the arc.
- Angular dimensions: the endpoints of the lines bounding the arc and the point used to select the arc.

In all these cases, the mid-point of the dimension text is also a definition point. The definition point positions are important because if an object is stretched, then the appropriate definition point must be included in the crossing for the dimension to be changed along with the entity.

There are three sub-commands which are specialized to operating on associative dimensions. These are:

UPDATE: edits existing dimension entities and converts them to the current settings of dimension variables, text style and units.

HOMETEXT: restores text to its normal position if it has become displaced during editing.

NEWTEXT: changes the dimension text in existing dimensions.

Each of these three commands returns 'Select object:' and so they can be used to modify several dimensions. In the extreme case, all associative dimensions on a drawing can be modified by using a window to create the selection set; other entities will not be selected.

A list of dimension variables will be found in Appendix B.

Exercises

1 Fully dimension each of the drawings that you completed in Exercise 1 of Chapter 3. Take care to adjust the arrow and text sizes to suit your taste.

2 Reproduce Figure 11.1.

3 Reproduce Figure 11.7, adding
   (a) bilateral tolerances of plus or minus 0.3 mm to the axial dimensions and
   (b) maximum/minimum limits of 0.2 mm to the dimensions of the cylindrical features.

4 Sometimes it is difficult to calculate clearances where the contributing tolerances do not act in the same direction. A simple example of this is in the plate shown in Figure 11.15a, where it is required to find the minimum material between the hole and the sloping side. This can be done quite neatly using the **STRETCH** facility. The procedure is shown in Figures 11.15b to 11.15h. Follow the example through.

12 Drawing enhancement

A description of AutoCAD polylines and the facilities for editing them, also the method used for drawing isometrics and sketching. The commands covered are **PLINE**, **PEDIT**, **ISOPLANE** and **SKETCH**.

Introduction to polylines

You should now be able to draw any shape, no matter how complex, as long as it is composed of lines, arcs and circles. Each element of a drawing produced in this way is independent of the others. For instance, if we draw a rectangle using the **LINE** command, each of the four lines is a separate object even though they are joined dimensionally. We can erase any of the lines without affecting the others. Objects which have a independent existence with their own set of properties are called 'entities' (a term that we have been using informally up to now). An AutoCAD entity has a type (say, 'line') and properties (including, for a line, the coordinates of the start and end-points, its linetype and the associated colour). Lines, arcs and circles do not have a property of width so it is impossible to comply with BS 308's recommendation that the profiles of the component should be drawn in wider lines than other features on the drawing. As we have discussed, this can be arranged on the plot, if a multipen plotter is available, by assigning a wider pen size to a particular colour. It would be better, however, if we could directly assign the property of width to the lines used to draw the profile and full lines of the component. The image displayed on the screen would then resemble the plot more closely.

In AutoCAD, there is an entity more complex than the simple ones that we have been using up to now – this is the 'polyline'. A polyline is a single entity made up from a set of lines and arcs joined together at their endpoints. These lines and arcs are called 'segments' when used in this way and their points of connection are called 'vertices'. Polylines have width and so may be used to draw the wider lines that are required in engineering drafting. Wide polylines

142

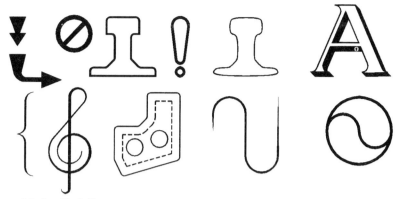

Figure 12.1 Polylines

are only filled in if the **FILL** command is used to set the system variable **FILLMODE** to **ON**. A variety of polylines is shown in Figure 12.1. Although the use of polylines is not so intuitively straightforward as that of simpler entities, they have, in suitable circumstances, very clear advantages.

- Each segment can be given a width which can vary uniformly throughout its length. It is unlikely that there will be a need for lines of variable thickness in practical engineering drawings but lines of constant width *are* useful.
- A polyline, no matter how complex, is a single entity and so it can be edited – for example, moved – in a single operation.
- A polyline is reliably connected. Often, a figure composed of lines, arcs and circles appears to be connected on the graphic display but, when it is magnified by a zoom, gaps and overlaps are seen to be present. This is due to the relatively coarse resolution of the screen. Lack of connectivity causes problems in operations such as hatching. If polylines are used to define hatch boundaries then hatching presents no difficulties.

Polylines with straight line segments

Polylines are drawn using the command **PLINE**. The initial command sequence is:

Command:**PLINE**
From point:

The start point of the polyline is then defined by being picked with the cursor or being typed in coordinate form. The sequence resumes:

Current line width is < some value >
Arc/Close/Halfwidth/Length/Undo/Width/< Endpoint of line >:

If you are drawing a line of constant width (as you generally are in engineering drafting) the width can be changed at this point by returning **Width** followed by the value. This is set until you change it again with another **Width** command. The option **Halfwidth** is useful in some circumstances but, since these are unlikely to occur in engineering drafting, it is probably better to forget it. If the polyline is composed only of linear segments, then using **PLINE** is very much like using **LINE**. An erroneous segment can be removed by selecting **Undo**; segments can be deleted successively and, if necessary, right back to the beginning of the sequence of lines; the polyline can be closed with a line segment by selecting **CLose**.

Example. Drawing a polyline with straight lines

Brief
Draw the polyline shown in Figure 12.2, making it 0.7 mm wide.

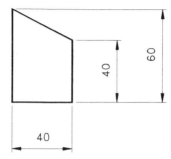

Figure 12.2   Example: Polylines with lines

Plan of Action
First make sure that the system variable **FILLMODE** is on by invoking the command **FILL**. Use **PLINE** and the sub-commands **Width** (and possibly **Undo**).

Command Sequence
    Command:**FILL**
    ON/OFF <OFF>:**ON**
    Command:**PLINE**
    From point:

Pick the start point of the polyline, then the command continues:

    Current line width is 0.00
    Arc/Close/Halfwidth/Length/Undo/Width/<Endpoint of line>:**W**
    Starting width <0.0000>:**0.7**
    Ending width <0.7000>:**RETURN**
    Arc/Close/Halfwidth/Length/Undo/Width/<Endpoint of line>:**@40,0**
    Arc/Close/Halfwidth/Length/Undo/Width/<Endpoint of line>:**@0,40**
    Arc/Close/Halfwidth/Length/Undo/Width/<Endpoint of line>:**@-40,20**
    Arc/Close/Halfwidth/Length/Undo/Width/<Endpoint of line>:**C**
    Command:

The **Close** sub-command terminates **PLINE**. If an open polyline is needed, then you can terminate with **CTRL-C** or **RETURN** when the polyline is complete. If you mistype a coordinate, then you can retrieve

---

the situation by using **Undo** which removes the previous segment and can be repeated if necessary.

Notice that the polyline shows up on the screen in a wider line than lines from the **LINE** command. You may have noticed that in the preceding diagrams, some of the lines were thicker than others. This was in the interests of clarity. You can now emphasize the lines on your own drawings.

Polylines with arcs

Drawing arc segments is rather more complicated than drawing lines. All segments are anchored to the endpoint of the previous segment. A line segment needs just one further pair of numbers to define it completely – for instance, the coordinates of the endpoint or the length of the line and the angle that it makes with some datum line. The definition of an arc is more complex since, in addition to the start point, four numbers are needed and many combinations are possible. If the response to the standard **PLINE** prompt is **Angle**, then the prompt becomes:

Angle/CEntre/CLose/Direction/Halfwidth/Line/Radius/Second pt/ Undo/Width/<Endpoint of arc>:

This prompt will be returned until a line segment is needed. The option **Line** is then selected and the prompt is switched. The actions of **Undo**, **CLose**, **Width** and **Halfwidth** are the same as in Line mode except that **CLose** completes the polyline with an arc rather than a line segment.

Endpoint of arc is the default. An arc segment will be drawn in an anticlockwise direction, starting at the endpoint of the last segment of the polyline and finishing with the input endpoint. Two points are insufficient to define an arc but, by default, the tangent to the arc starts at the ending tangent angle of the last segment defined. If the last segment is a line, then the arc will be drawn so that the last line is tangential to it. If **Drag** is on, then the form of the potential arc is visible before the user is actually committed to the endpoint, which is a useful aid.

If the arc is not satisfactory – for instance, if it needs to be drawn clockwise – then a **Direction** can be defined by entering a point. The arc will be drawn with its starting direction towards the point. If the arc is the first segment of the polyline, then its direction will be that of the line, arc or polyline segment drawn prior to the **PLINE** command. If you must start a polyline with an arc segment, then it is better to define its direction explicitly using the **Direction** option.

The other combinations are similar to those (shown in Figure 6.4) for the simple **ARC** command; examples are:

Angle and endpoint   Radius and endpoint
Angle and CEntre   Second point and endpoint
Angle and Radius
CEntre and endpoint
CEntre and Angle
CEntre and Length (of chord)

A common drafting requirement is drawing an isolated circle. This may be done in various ways, for example:

Command:**PLINE**
From point:**Pick a point on the circumference**
Arc/Close/Halfwidth/Length/Undo/Width/<Endpoint of line>:**A**
Angle/CEntre/CLose/Direction/Halfwidth/Line/Radius/Second pt/
Undo/Width/<Endpoint of arc>:**CE**
Centre point:**Pick the centre point**
Angle/Length/<Endpoint>:**Pick another point on the circle**
Angle/CEntre/CLose/Direction/Halfwidth/Line/Radius/Second pt/
Undo/Width/<Endpoint of arc>:**CL**
Angle/CEntre/CLose/Direction/Halfwidth/Line/Radius/Second pt/
Undo/Width/<Endpoint of arc>:**RETURN**
Command:

It is easier, however, to draw a circular polyline using the command **DONUT** (described in Chapter 6), which acts directly.

Command:**DONUT**
Inside diameter<0.00>:**Enter diameter minus width**
Outside diameter<1.00>:**Enter diameter plus width**
Center of donut:**Pick the center of the circle**
Center of donut:**RETURN**

The command is very useful in the common case when several holes of the same diameter are to be drawn. Again, in order to fill the polyline which results, **FILLMODE** must be **ON**.

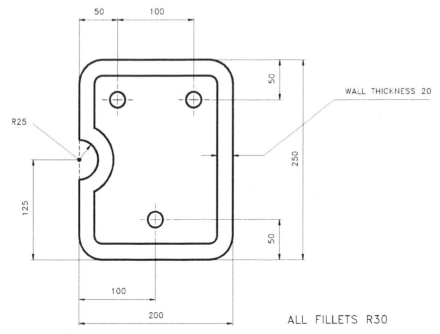

Figure 12.3 Example: Polylines with arcs

Example. **A polyline containing arc segments**

Brief
Draw the part shown in Figure 12.3.

Plan of action
Make sure that **FILLMODE** is **ON**. Use a closed polyline for the outside boundary and doughnuts for the holes. Start at the top left corner whose coordinates are {100, 300}.

Command sequence
```
Command:PLINE
From point:100,300
Arc/Close/Halfwidth/Length/Undo/Width/<Endpoint of line>:W
Starting width<0.0000>:0.7
Ending width<0.7000>RETURN
Arc/Close/Halfwidth/Length/Undo/Width/<Endpoint of line>:
@0,-100
Arc/Close/Halfwidth/Length/Undo/Width/<Endpoint of line>:A
Angle/CEntre/CLose/Direction/Halfwidth/Line/Radius/Second pt/
Undo/Width/<Endpoint of arc>:D
Direction from starting point:Fix direction by eg @10,0
Endpoint:@0,-50
Angle/CEntre/CLose/Direction/Halfwidth/Line/Radius/Second pt/
Undo/Width/<Endpoint of arc>:L
Arc/Close/Halfwidth/Length/Undo/Width/<Endpoint of line>:
@0,-100
Arc/Close/Halfwidth/Length/Undo/Width/<Endpoint of line>:
@200,0
Arc/Close/Halfwidth/Length/Undo/Width/<Endpoint of line>:
@0,250
Arc/Close/Halfwidth/Length/Undo/Width/<Endpoint of line>:
@-200,0
Arc/Close/Halfwidth/Length/Undo/Width/<Endpoint of line>:
C
Arc/Close/Halfwidth/Length/Undo/Width/<Endpoint of line>:
RETURN
Command:DONUT
Inside diameter<0.50>:20.7
Outside diameter<4.00>:19.3
Center of donut:150,250
Center of donut:250,250
Center of donut:200,100
Center of donut:RETURN
Command:
```

The remainder of the drawing: text, dimensions, the wall (use **OFFSET**) are left to you.

Editing polylines

Polylines can be edited in the same way as other entities; they can be erased, moved, rotated, copied and so on. The only difference between editing a polyline and other types of entity by these operations is that it is often easier to edit a polyline. Since it is an entity, just one pick on any part of it sends *all* the segments to the selection set. There is a difficulty, however. Since a polyline is an entity, it is impossible to edit one segment in isolation by any of the normal editing procedures. It is a case of 'edit one, edit all'. If we do wish to change any of the segments, then we must dismember the polyline by means of the **EXPLODE** command. Each segment is then converted to a separate entity and can be dealt with separately. Unfortunately, one of the major advantages of using polylines is lost if **EXPLODE** is used. The lines no longer have width. You can, however, later reconvert the separate entities to a polyline by **PEDIT**. This inconvenient procedure may be avoided by either *planning ahead* or, in most cases, by using directly the facilities offered by **PEDIT**. If we wish to edit a polyline as a whole, rather than **EXPLODE**ing it, the command **PEDIT** returns the prompts:

Select polyline:**The polyline to edited is picked**
Close/Join/Width/Edit vertex/Fit curve/Spline curve/Decurve
/Undo/eXit<X>:

The command is terminated if **eXit** (or **X**) is returned. The option **Close** closes an open polyline; if the selected polyline happens to be closed already, then the **Close** prompt is replaced by **Open**.

Undo reverses the previous editing command and, if it is used repeatedly, all the editing operations performed during the current **PEDIT** can be reversed.

The remaining options may be separated into two groups – those which operate on a whole polyline and those which operate on individual segments, the latter being activated by picking the option **Edit vertex**.

Some useful actions operating on the whole polyline are shown in Figure 12.4.

The **Width** option allows you to change the width of an existing polyline. When **Width** is selected, the system prompts for a value and the whole polyline is set to that uniform width.

Fit curve constructs a smooth curve consisting of two arcs between each adjacent pair of vertices.

Spline curve uses the vertices of the polyline as the control points for a spline curve. Spline curves are more visually pleasant than curves made up from arcs; they are, however, more difficult to dimension. There are two kinds of spline curve available in AutoCAD – Quadratic B-splines and Cubic B-splines. The type of spline curve is determined by a number assigned to the system variable **SPLINETYPE**. If this is set to 5, then a quadratic B-spline will be drawn. If it is set to 6, then a cubic B-spline will result. The smoothness of the curve is affected by a value given to the system variable **SPLINESEGS**. This defaults to 8, which gives reasonably satisfactory results. A higher value will result in longer processing times and bigger drawing files.

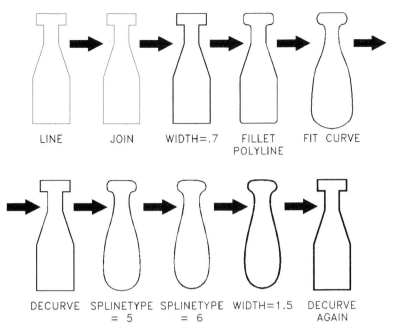

LINE   JOIN   WIDTH=.7   FILLET   FIT CURVE
                                         POLYLINE

DECURVE   SPLINETYPE   SPLINETYPE   WIDTH=1.5   DECURVE
              = 5   = 6   AGAIN

Figure 12.4   Editing a polyline

Traditionally, engineering shapes are made up from lines and arcs. This is probably because of the processes traditionally available for manufacturing engineering artefacts. With the advent of numerically controlled machines and CAM programs, the use of freer forms may become commonplace. There is an essential difference in dimensioning between shapes defined by line and arc and those defined by more complex forms. Lines and arcs can be dimensioned easily and precisely by conventional means – length and angle, and centre and radius, for example. Spline curves are mathematically defined and their practical definition is commonly a set of NC commands. The only place for traditional dimensions when spline curves are used is the provision of a set of check coordinates for gauging purposes. Good drafting practice in this case is not dealt with in current drafting standards. Using splines is not an intuitive activity and needs a good deal of practice. A detailed discussion of spline curves may be found in *Computer Graphics: An Introduction to the Mathematics and Geometry* by M. E. Mortenson (Butterworth-Heinemann, UK; Industrial Press, USA).

Both **Fit curve** and **Spline curve** can be reversed by the option **Decurve** which returns the polyline to a form made up from straight line segments. If the polyline had arc segments before **PEDIT** was entered, then they will be lost, each vertex pair now being joined by a straight line.

Probably the most useful option in everyday drafting is **Join**. This is used to convert separate connected entities into single polylines. Even if you do not wish to take advantage of the width feature of polylines and are content to construct shapes from line and arc entities, it is handy to convert the boundaries of section hatches into polylines, since this results in the system being able to find the limits of the hatch unambiguously. We shall return to this in the next section. If the option **Join** is selected, then the prompt returned is:

Select objects:

The operator can then, as usual with this prompt, create a selection set of objects: lines, arcs and polylines which are candidates for merging into one polyline. Objects selected must be exactly connected. In ambiguous cases, the system selects arbitrarily one of the possible candidates. For this reason, it is usually better to select individual entities than to use the **Window** option.

Editing vertices

Vertex editing may involve one vertex or a pair of vertices. On entry to **Edit vertex**, the system replies:

Next/Previous/Break/Insert/Move/Regen/Straighten/Tangent/Width/ eXit<N>:

Also, the first vertex of the polyline is marked with a cross. This is the current vertex which can be moved along the polyline by using the commands **Next** and **Previous**.

The command **Break** results in the prompt:

Next/Previous/Go/eXit<N>:

The current vertex on entry is taken as the first point of a break in the polyline and the marker can now be driven round the vertices of the polyline to find the second point. When this has been marked, input of **Go** results in the polyline being dissected into two separate polylines. If one vertex is at the end of the polyline then the part between the vertices will be removed and the polyline will finish up shorter, but still connected. If both end vertices are chosen, then an error message will result. If you change your mind about breaking the polyline, then **eXit** will return you to the main prompt again.

The command **Insert** permits you to add a new vertex to the polyline. This will be between two existing vertices, the current vertex (marked with a cross) and the vertex after it. The new vertex is joined by straight segments to the vertices on each side of it. If the user returns **Insert**, then the system responds:

Enter location of new vertex:

The point is then picked and the polyline altered.

Move allows you to change the location of the current vertex. Its prompt line is:

Enter new location:

Regen regenerates the polyline.

Straighten acts like **Break**, but the portions of the original polyline are not converted into two separate polylines. They are joined by a straight line segment. Again, the vertex on entry to the option is taken as the first vertex to be joined by the line. The second endpoint is chosen by picking from the prompt menu:

Next/Previous/Go/eXit<N>:

On selection of **Go**, the vertices between the two selected vertices are deleted and the two selected vertices joined by a line segment.

Tangent is used to add a tangent angle to the current vertex. The resultant prompt is:

Direction of tangent:

As with the **Direction** prompt from the **PLINE** command, the angle can be input explicitly or can be indicated by picking a point.

Width allows the segment between the current marked vertex and the vertex immediately following to be allocated a starting and an ending width. In this case, the change of width is not carried out immediately and **Regen** is needed if you wish to see the results of your editing so far.

The option **eXit** returns you to the **PEDIT** prompt.

There are other commands that affect polylines. The only one that is of common application is the **Polyline** option in **FILLET**. A whole polyline can have its adjoining vertices filleted in just one command using this option. An example of its use is shown in Figure 12.4.

Introduction to isometric projection

The objective of engineering drafting, either manual or computer aided, is to represent a three-dimensional body on a two-dimensional surface in a way that is precisely defined and which helps visualization of the body. The conventional engineering drawing can be used to specify the geometric form of most engineering parts (although occasionally one gets the impression that a part has been given a form *because* it is specifiable by conventional engineering drawing methods). Though there are occasional difficulties of representation, engineering has been around long enough for methods of coping with them to have evolved. The problem of visualization is rather more difficult. If an object has a complex form, it is not easy for an inexperienced viewer to picture it intuitively from a conventional engineering drawing.

Computer surface and solid modelling systems produce drawings which aid visualization very well indeed and have other advantages over the conventional engineering drawing. The penalty with current three-dimensional modelling systems is that definition of a particularly complex object is very time consuming and, in some cases, it may even be impossible. Many authorities have claimed for years that conventional drafting will be supplanted eventually by three-dimensional modelling but, judging by the number of two-dimensional drafting systems being sold, this does not yet seem to happening to any great degree.

There are other kinds of projection which, though not so suited to the *definition* of a body as is two-dimensional drafting, give more help in *visualizing* a component's shape from a drawing. The most commonly used in engineering is the isometric projection. Isometrics are not normally used to specify the dimensions of a form but as auxiliary representations which help interpretation.

Projections other than isometric are also used for this purpose. The most realistic way of representing a solid on a flat surface is the perspective drawing. This is not used very often in engineering applications because, although a perspective can be constructed geometrically (there are some proprietary devices to do this mechanically), it takes a good deal of time to draw an accurate perspective of a complicated form. Moreover, the fore-shortening effect of perspective tends to obscure detail. For these reasons, perspective projection has not been used much in engineering communication. There may, however, be an increase in its popularity with the development of programs such as AutoCAD which allow a body to be defined in three dimensions and viewed from any direction in true perspective. If an object is at all complex, it is probably better and easier to use a three-dimensional modelling system such as AutoSolid.

Non-perspective projections are called parallel projections; these were mentioned briefly in Chapter 3. Examples of parallel projections are:

- The oblique projections, Cabinet and Cavalier being popular in architectural drawing. Oblique projections are also used occasionally in engineering drawing but they give a poor representation for circular detail on faces not parallel to the picture plane.
- The orthographic projections, among which are a family called axonometric (isometric being among these) and the multiview projections, first and third angle.

All projections apart from perspective are approximations to realism and although isometric drawings are not exact geometrical representations, they look 'right' for most forms. Some examples are shown in Figures 3.7a–f (page 31).

Isometric drawing in AutoCAD

There is a special snap grid in AutoCAD which enables isometrics to be constructed quickly and accurately. This is turned on by using the option in **SNAP** that was glossed over in Chapter 5. The command sequence is:

Command:**SNAP**
Snap spacing or ON/OFF/Aspect/Rotate/Style < current > :**STYLE**
Standard/Isometric < current style > :**I**
Vertical spacing < current value > :**Enter value**

An isometric grid is now available – this can now be switched on and off by using the **GRID** command or, more conveniently, using the toggle **CTRL-G**. The dots on the isometric grid are not in a raster form but aligned along three axes at 30 degrees, 90 degrees and 150 degrees to the horizontal. These are isometric projections of the three normal coordinate axes in Cartesian coordinates. 'Isometric' means 'of equal measure' and distances can be measured along the isometric axes on an equal scale. As in all projections, a body can be projected in any position and orientation, but it is usual to place the body in a position which takes maximum advantage of the equal scaling property. This position is where known dimensions on the body correspond with measurements along the isometric axes – Figures 3.7a to 3.7f illustrate the principle.

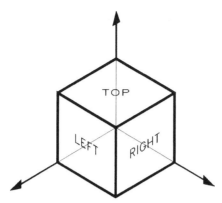

Figure 12.5 Isometric planes

It is usual to refer dimensions on the body to a bounding cuboid. In Figure 12.5 are shown the three isometric planes: Left, Top and Right. The crosshair of the drawing cursor is adjusted in isometric snap so that its lines can lie along any pair of the isometric axes:

90 and 150 degrees   Left plane.
150 and   30 degrees   Top plane.
30 and   90 degrees   Right plane.

The crosshair can be switched from one to another of these by using the command:

Command:**ISOPLANE**
Left/Top/Right/(Toggle):

If **RETURN** is entered, the next plane in the cyclic sequence: Left > Top > Right > Left > ... is selected. A cyclic switch can be made more conveniently by using **CTRL-E**.

Circles become ellipses in isometric projection. If you have selected isometric snap, an extra option is supplied with the command **ELLIPSE**:

Command:**ELLIPSE**
<Axis endpoint 1>/Centre/Isocircle:**I**
Centre of circle:**Enter centre on isometric plane**
<Circle radius>/Diameter:**Enter radius**

This draws the ellipse in the form appropriate to the current isoplane.

Example. **Isometrics**

Brief
Construct an isometric drawing of the body shown in Figure 12.6.

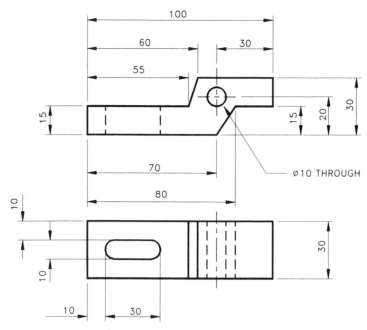

Figure 12.6 Example: Isometric drawing

Plan of action
Select an isometric snap of 5 mm on a 10 mm grid. Select a suitable orientation and draw the bounding cuboid – 30 × 30 × 100 mm – on the construction layer. Use the cuboid to draw the straight edges on the drawing layer. This can be done without any reference to an isoplane. Finally, draw the slot on the top isoplane and the hole on the right isoplane. The process is shown in Figure 12.7.

Command sequence
If you are using our standard prototype drawing, switch the construction layer on and make it current. Otherwise, you will have to create a new layer. Then set up the snap grid.

Command:**SNAP**
Snap spacing or ON/OFF/Aspect/Rotate/Style < current > :**5**
Command:**RETURN**
Snap spacing or ON/OFF/Aspect/Rotate/Style < 5.0 > **S**
Standard/Isometric < Standard > :**I**
Vertical spacing < 5.0 > **5**
Command:**GRID**
Grid spacing(X) or ON/OFF/Snap/Aspect < current > :**10**
Command:**CTRL-G CTRL-B LINE**
First point:

Now draw the bounding cuboid by picking points on the grid. If you toggle to the correct isoplane, you can use the dimension read-out to check the position of your cursor; in this case, it is easy enough to count the dots along the grid. You should arrive at the display shown in Figure 12.7a.

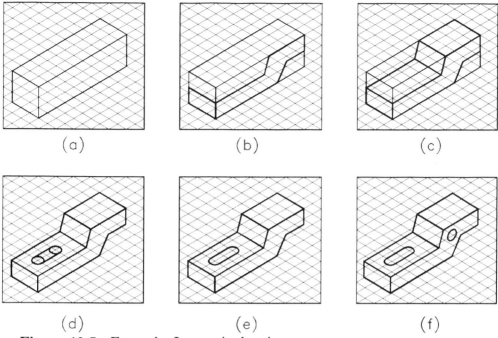

Figure 12.7   Example: Isometric drawing

Next switch on the drawing layer and make it current. Draw the form shown in stages shown in Figures 12.7b and c.

Switch to the top isoplane and draw two circles at the end of the slot.

Command:**ISOPLANE**
Left/Top/Right/(Toggle):**T**
Command:**ELLIPSE**
<Axis endpoint 1>/Centre/Isocircle:**I**
Centre of circle:**Pick centre of circle**
<Circle radius>/Diameter:**Pick point on circumference**
Command:**RETURN**
<Axis endpoint 1>/Centre/Isocircle:**I**
Centre of circle:**Pick centre of other circle**
<Circle radius>/Diameter:**Pick point on circumference**
Command:

Now draw the lines on the slot (Figure 12.7d). Zoom into a window around the slot. The isocircles are polylines which must be edited and therefore need to be first exploded. They now become separate arc segments which can be edited separately. Erase the unwanted bits – you will find that this is not too difficult since AutoDesk have considerably arranged the arc segments so that some of them end on quadrant points, making an isometric semicircle easy to create. Your drawing should now look like Figure 12.7e.

Transfer to the right isoplane by using **ISOPLANE** or the toggle **CTRL-E** and draw the circle. Switch off the construction layer. Your drawing should now look like Figure 12.7f.

Sketching

Although component drawings are drawn strictly to scale, there are occasional applications of freehand sketching in engineering drafting. An example is the ragged line used in the broken section shown in Figure 11.13a (page 133). AutoCAD provides an elementary sketching facility for such applications. This is difficult to use for anything complex unless your graphics input device is a tablet and stylus and even then it needs a fair amount of practice to get good results. The command sequence for initiating the sketching facility is:

Command:**SKETCH**
Record increment < current > ;

The sketch will be made up from lines, usually short, of a length equal to the record increment. A sketch consists of one or more continuous sequences of lines. A sequence can be made up of separate line entities if the system variable **SKPOLY** is zero or can be a polyline if **SKPOLY** is set to a non-zero value. The system variable is set using the command **SETVAR**. It is important to keep the record increment as large as possible since it is very easy (and very tempting) to use up storage space rapidly. On an A4 sheet of 297 mm by 210 mm, a record increment not less than 2 mm should be adequate for most purposes. As the sketch progresses, previous sections can be 'recorded' or stored away when they are considered satisfactory. When the record increment has been input in drawing units, the system replies with the prompt:

Sketch. Pen eXit Quit Record Erase Connect .

Notice that the format of this prompt line is different from the usual Auto-CAD standard prompt. This is because the sketch facility is really a sub-system embedded in AutoCAD and is quite unlike the other operations. AutoCAD also market a separate sketching system, AutoSketch, and the facility is a miniature version of it.

The commands simulate the drawing action of a pen which can be raised or lowered by using the **Pen** (or **P**) subcommand. None of the sketching commands require a **RETURN**; they are activated just by typing or picking the command (or its abbreviated form). The pointing device should be moved to the start of the sketch, **P** input (or the pick button of the graphics input device pressed) and the first continuous set of lines drawn by moving the pointing device, freely tracking its position visually on the screen. Only when the pen has moved a distance from the last point equal to the record increment is a line drawn, and this lag in drawing is quite discomfiting if the record increment is too large. Some compromise is needed: too large an increment and the freehand sketching becomes a difficult process because of the lag; too small an increment and you are liable to use up all your disk space. When the first set of lines has been drawn, another **P** is input to raise the pen. The cursor can then be moved to another point and the process repeated.

The sets of lines shown are shown in a distinctive colour if you have a colour system, and they are not yet stored permanently (or 'recorded'). A section of sketch *can* be recorded, if you are satisfied with it, by inputting **Record** (or **R**). This does not change the state of the pen. If at any stage you want to store the whole sketch, **X** records all the lines currently entered and leaves the **SKETCH** sub-system. **Q** discards all unrecorded lines and again returns to the normal AutoCAD 'Command:' prompt.

Sketches can be edited during the course of the command by input of **E**. This command raises the pen, if necessary, and allows you to erase part of a line set by picking an intermediate point. The line set is then erased from the point picked to the end of the last record increment. If you interrupt the sketching of a line set by raising the pen or doing some other action, then you can resume sketching where you left off by input of **C**. The desired endpoint, either of the last line set or the end of an erased line set, must then be picked and sketching can carry on. Input of a full stop will result in a line being drawn from the end of the last line set to the current pen position.

Sketching in this way is hardly a natural activity. The commands are easy to use, but the problem is drawing the sketch by remote control. This is not too difficult a process if, as we have remarked, the pointing device is a stylus;

Figure 12.8   Use of SKETCH

since the feedback seems more direct compared with that obtained from using a mouse. This may be because a stylus is more like a normal drawing implement than is a mouse. But if a mouse is used, you must be prepared for some bizarre results before you achieve proficiency. The crude facial detail in Figure 13.1 (page 162) was drawn using a stylus and tablet. A zoomed detail is shown in Figure 12.8.

Exercises

1   Reproduce the isometrics shown in Figure 3.7 (page 31).

2   Experiment with the **SKETCH** facility by trying to reproduce your normal signature. Try different record increments but don't make them so small that they use up all your disk. (*Note.* If this should happen, then you will not lose all your drawings. AutoCAD warns you so that you can take remedial action. This should never occur; at all times, you should keep storage under control by erasing obsolete drawings from the hard disk, frequent back-ups and storage accountancy.)

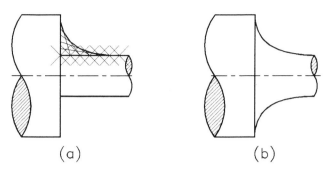

Figure 12.9   Constructing a fairing

3   Figure 12.9 shows a technique for drawing a hyperbolic fairing such as is found on aircraft wings. The envelope is obtained by connecting points generated by a **DIVIDE** on both of the lines which are to be faired off. Use a polyline to bound the envelope, then use **PEDIT** to convert the polyline to a quadratic spline curve.

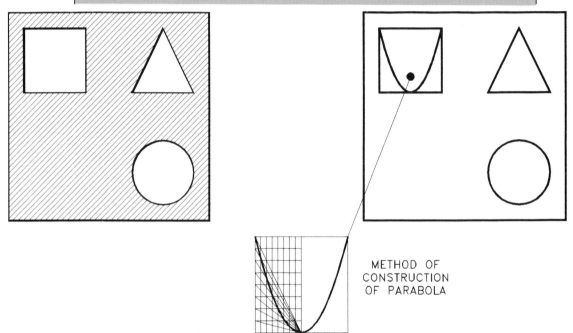

METHOD OF
CONSTRUCTION
OF PARABOLA

Figure 12.10   Use of spline curves

4   Figure 12.10 shows a common drawing office puzzle. The problem is to design a plug which will pass exactly through each of the holes in the plate. The holes are in the forms of a square, a triangle and a circle. The parabolic form on the side view is obtained by generating an envelope as in Exercise 3 and converting it to a quadratic spline curve.

<table>
<tr>
<td>

13

</td>
<td>

Blocks and attributes

</td>
</tr>
</table>

A description of the application, definition and retrieval of blocks is followed by a discussion of the AutoCAD attribute facility. Commands covered include **BLOCK, WBLOCK, INSERT, BASE, MINSERT, ATTDEF, ATTEDIT, DDATTE** and **ATTDISP.**

Introduction to blocks

In AutoCAD, entities are not simply elementary objects such as lines, arcs and circles. In previous sections, we have been using polylines which are composed of groups of elementary objects; associative dimensions are lines and text together with definition points which control their positions. Another complex entity is the block. A block consists of an assembly of other entities (possibly including other blocks), an insertion base point and some associated text. Once a block has been defined, it can be stored, retrieved and placed anywhere on a drawing. The motivation for using blocks is economy – economy of both drawing time and storage.

In engineering drafting, a fair proportion of time is spent in drawing standard and conventional objects. For instance, most general assemblies show fasteners: bolts, nuts, studs, washers and rivets. To draw these in detail would be a time-wasting process. It is convenient to have them predefined so that the drafter can draw them by just referring to them by name and indicating the position at which they are to be drawn. The resulting representations are precise and standardized. All fields of engineering use specialized symbols to communicate information and it is possible to buy sets of predefined symbols for many applications in AutoCAD. These are often supplied on iconized menu cards.

There are many standard marks commonly used on drawings: projection symbols, machining and surface texture symbols are examples. Many countries have their own national standard for drawing symbols and their use on drawings is so frequent that it is worthwhile to spend time in predefining them as blocks.

The benefits resulting from using blocks for such applications are clear.

- Using blocks results in representations that are precisely scaled and in an acceptable standard form.
- Drafters can be forced to use a preferred range of components; this is normally highly desirable.
- The time taken to draw standard components is considerably reduced.
- Since a block is stored in the drawing file as a reference to the stored definition rather than as the individual entities, drawing files can be smaller.
- Drawings may be built up in sections. For instance, in tool drawing, it is common practice to show all the details on a large drawing sheet. It is convenient to define each detail separately as a block. This takes advantage of standard details and introduces parallelism into drawing, so that more than one drafter can work on the same job.

In addition to the drawn entities, a block contains one reference point, called the insertion base point, which is used to locate the block on the drawing on which it is to be placed. Textual information (or 'attributes') can also be stored in the block definition. Attributes can, for example, hold part numbers of a component. The drawing file may then be processed so that these attributes can be extracted and parts lists built up automatically. Attributes will be dealt with at a later stage.

Defining blocks in AutoCAD

Blocks can be defined by using the command sequence:

Command:**BLOCK**
Block name (or ?):**Type block name**
Insertion base point:**Pick insertion point**
Select objects:**Pick objects to include in the block**

This command sequence defines blocks which are to be used in the current drawing. If they are to be used subsequently in other drawings, then **BLOCK** is replaced by **WBLOCK**. The block name is user-defined and, as usual, it is sound practice to make the chosen name as descriptive and mnemonic as possible. It is not very helpful to christen a block representing a particular size of bolt 'BOLTG'; 'BOLT—M10' is a more descriptive and easily remembered name. Since block names can be 31 characters long, and contain letters, numbers, the dollar sign, hyphens ('-') and underlines ('__'), there is no excuse for making block names other than descriptive.

If a block with the name supplied is in existence already, then the system replies

Block <Block name> already exists.
Redefine it?<N>:

RETURN or **N** results in the command being aborted with no action being taken. If **Y** is input, then the definition proceeds.

If **?** is input, then (as you might guess by this time) a list of all the blocks defined in the drawing is produced.

When a block is retrieved, the user is prompted for an insertion base point, which is the datum at which the block will be placed. The corresponding point must be established when the block is defined. The defined block has a local coordinate system with its insertion base point as origin and the directions of its coordinates parallel with the UCS in force at the time of definition. This means that a block can be retrieved at any orientation by rotating the UCS before retrieval.

The component entities of the block are picked in the usual way by building a selection set. When the selection set has been satisfactorily created, the block is defined. Selected entities are deleted from both the screen and the drawing but, if they are needed for subsequent work, then they may be restored by **OOPS**.

WBLOCK acts in broadly the same way as **BLOCK**. The command sequence is

Command:**WBLOCK**
Filename:**Input filename**
Block name:**Input block name**

The block has two names: the filename, by which it is known to the operating system, and the block name, by which it is known to the the drawing. Although the filename is restricted to, usually, eight characters, it is worthwhile trying to make this as mnemonic as possible also. The block is filed under the name which has been supplied with the extension '.DWG' automatically added. The extension should not be included in the input filename. A consequence of this procedure is that any drawing, regardless of its complexity, can be retrieved as a block.

There are several ways to respond to the block name prompt. It may be that the block has already been defined in the current drawing using the **BLOCK** command. The prompt can be answered by the previously defined block name. This results in the block being stored and the command being abandoned.

If you choose to give the block the same name as the filename, then = saves you having to type it again. The response ★ defines the block as the whole drawing. This is not quite the same as **SAVE**, since the layer structure and other information which are part of a saved drawing are not retained – just the drawn marks. Input of **RETURN** results in a command sequence identical with that for **BLOCK**.

Example. **Defining a block**

Brief
Draw a symbol for third angle projection.

Plan of action
The symbol has already been discussed in Chapter 3. The recommended proportions for projection symbols are shown in Figure 13.1, which is taken from BSI publication PP7308. We shall take d = 5 mm which will

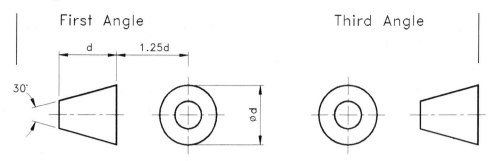

RECOMMENDED PROPORTIONS

Figure 13.1   Example: BLOCK definition

look in proportion on our standard drafting sheet A4SHEET. The insertion base point is conveniently defined at the centre of the circle.

Command sequence
Draw the symbol to the proportions given with d = 5. Then define it as a block by:

Command:**WBLOCK**
Filename:**PROJSYM3**
Block name:**Projection—symbol—3rd-angle**
Insertion base point:**Pick the centre – OSNAP CEN perhaps?**
Select objects:**W**
First corner:**Pick bottom left**
Other corner:**Pick top right**
Select objects:**RETURN**

The drawing will disappear from the screen and the block will be stored for further use. Note that the block name has been defined differently from the filename. This is not really necessary in this case since we need not use the block any more on the current drawing. It has been included to show an example of a descriptive block name (possibly the description has been overdone in this case). It is useful to try to retrieve the block a few times so as to confirm that it has been correctly defined.

Retrieving blocks in AutoCAD

The command **INSERT** can be used to retrieve a block and place it in position on a drawing. The command sequence is:

Command:**INSERT**
Block name(or ?):**Input block name**
Insertion point:**Pick the position of the block**
X scale factor<1>/Corner/XYZ:**Input scale factor**
Y scale factor<default=X>:**Input scale if different from X**
Rotation angle<0>:**Input angle, if needed**

The block is drawn so that its defined insertion base point is located at the picked insertion point. It may be scaled in both X and Y directions and may be rotated about the insertion point by an input angle. Usually scales and angles are input numerically, but it is possible to pick them with the cursor. Scales may be defined by selecting the **Corner** option and picking a point above and to the right of the insertion point, the sides of the box so formed determining the X and Y scales. This is particularly useful if the block has been defined to lie inside a box with unit sides. A negative scale factor will result in the block being both scaled and mirrored. In a like way, the angle of rotation can also be defined by a cursor pick; the rotation is then through the angle between the insertion point and the picked point. The scale option **XYZ** is used with three-dimensional blocks. Since we are only dealing with two-dimensional drawings here, you can ignore it.

If **DRAGMODE** is **ON**, then the block can be dragged to its desired position. A problem here is that the form being dragged may be dissimilar in scale and rotation to the form which will eventually be planted at the insertion point. If you do know the details of the final form prior to inserting it, then they may be set before insertion. Options are input at the **Insertion point** prompt which can refer either to the definite final values or to provisional values. These are:

SCale	**PS**cale
Xscale	**PX**scale
Yscale	**PY**scale
Zscale	**PZ**scale
Rotate	**PR**otate

Although these options are occasionally useful, they complicate the **INSERT** command. It is recommended that you ignore them until you have some experience of using the normal command sequence.

Since a block is an entity, its components cannot be edited separately. Its elements are not available in the drawing file. However, when using **INSERT**, if the block name is preceded by an asterisk the block will not be retrieved as an entity; its components will be written into the drawing file as independent objects. Although this does sacrifice one of the benefits of using blocks (their economy of storage), the individual components can then be edited as normal. If desired, they can then be redefined as a new block. The only restriction on retrieving blocks in this manner is that only one scale factor can be used. Another method of dismembering a block is to use the command **EXPLODE**.

A very useful feature of AutoCAD is being able to define whole drawings as blocks. For instance, component drawings can be defined as blocks and then combined to form a general assembly drawing. Input of the block name during the **INSERT** sequence initiates a search; if a block of that name has not been defined in the drawing, the system looks for a drawing file. If one is found with the right name, it is converted to a defined block in the drawing with insertion point, scale factors and rotation angle input as normal. The insertion base point is assumed to lie at the origin of the drawing coordinates. The new block will be drawn unless the user has returned **CTRL-C** when asked for the insertion point: in this case, the block is only defined in the current drawing and can be inserted later. The defined block can be given a name different from the drawing's name by using the construction:

Block name(or ?):**new-block-name = old-drawing-name**

When defining a whole drawing as a block, it may be inconvenient to have the origin as the insertion base point. Another point can be chosen by using the command **BASE** which prompts the user for an insertion base point. The drawing may subsequently be defined by **BLOCK** or filed as a block by **WBLOCK**.

Arrays of blocks can be drawn by using the **MINSERT** command. This acts like the **ARRAY** command except that a block name is input rather than a selection set defined.

Applications of blocks

Many of the objects on a drawing are conventional symbols; they are not geometrically exact representations but are simplified forms that are universally recognized. Although the precise forms of these conventional symbols are usually defined by national standards, they do not vary so much that the representation of, say, a bolt drawn to a European standard would be unintelligible to an American engineer. There is a prevailing movement towards unification of standards and so these symbols form a type of engineering universal language.

Not only does the use of conventional symbols aid communication, it also saves a good deal of drafting time. Also, because all superfluous detail is omitted, the clarity of a drawing is improved.

As an example, consider a bolt, probably the most common of machine elements. Figure 13.2 shows three representations. Although (a) shows a simplified form of the thread, it involves a lot of drawing time and would only be used for special applications such as technical illustrations. Form (b) has been abstracted further and is sometimes used, especially in the USA.

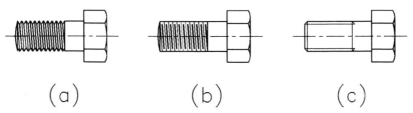

(a)   (b)   (c)

Figure 13.2   Representations of a bolt

The most common representation is (c), which is also the simplest. It is not usually necessary to draw even this simplified form precisely to scale, since it is unusual for anyone to need to scale details such as the minor diameter of the thread. The most abstract form of representation is the textual note: simple fixings such as rivets are often not drawn at all, just their centrelines being indicated in the conventional way and a note added to describe them. It is unusual for drawings to carry this principle very far, however, and the conventional symbols that engineering drafters use normally resemble the object being represented.

A good selection of conventional representations is given in BS 308 Part 1. Some of the more useful are shown in Appendix A. Other British Standards give lists of graphical symbols used in specialized fields, some being:

BS 1553   Graphical symbols for general engineering Part 1 Graphical symbols for piping systems and plant.

BS 2917   Specification for graphical symbols used on diagrams for fluid power systems and components.

BS 3939   Graphical symbols for electrical power, telecommunications and electronics diagrams.

Since AutoCAD is so widely used, it is possible to buy sets of symbols for most specialized applications.

Example. **A block to represent a conventional engineering symbol**

Brief
Define a standard ISO nut as a block.

Plan of action
The form of an ISO nut is shown in Figure 13.3. We really need three blocks to represent the plan view, the side view across the corners and the side view across the flats. The dimensions of a standard nut do not bear an exact linear relationship with the nominal thread size but there is an approximate relation which is reasonable. This, for smaller sizes, gives a nut which is too small, but unless we are interested in spanner clearances or other applications requiring exact dimensions, it is pictorially adequate. If sufficient time were available, then it would be better to define blocks for each size of nut separately.

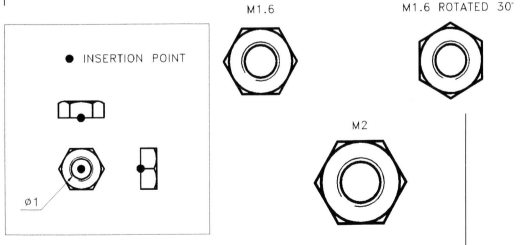

Figure 13.3   Example: Block for a nut

If the nominal thread diameter is d, then the size of nut or bolt head is given by:

Diameter across the flats   1.5d
Head thickness (nut)   0.8d
Head thickness (bolt)   0.7d

It is convenient in the plan view to define the insertion base point as the centre of the hole. In the side views, the most convenient positions are as shown in Figure 13.3. In this case, it advantageous to draw the nut for a value of d = 1 mm, since then the scale on insertion will give the correct size of nut.

If you do decide to draw the side views also, you can find procedures for drawing the radii in specialized drafting texts. Perfectly satisfactory results can be obtained by using your judgement – the radii are only approximations, anyway. In manual drafting, it is customary to show the 30 degrees chamfer across the corners on the side view of the nut. In computer aided drafting, we recommend that you forget it.

It was possible to define a block for *all* ISO nuts because they are geometrically similar and their dimensions have an approximate linear relationship with the thread diameter. The same is not, however, true for bolts. Heads of bolts can be defined in the same way as nuts so the plan view is easily handled. But the side view of all bolts is not even approximately geometrically similar. The threaded and unthreaded length, undercuts and other features all have an independent existence. It is impossible, then, to define a standard block for all bolts. This does not mean that bolts need be painstakingly drawn, however. It is possible, using the AutoLisp interpreter supplied with AutoCAD, to define a generalized bolt so that the variable parameters can be input and the bolt drawn automatically.

Although we have defined a block which will represent all nuts approximately, this approach, though neat, has some drawbacks. As we have mentioned, the smaller sizes will look too small to an experienced eye. A more important snag, however, is that there is no restriction on the size of nut that can be drawn. We would not be prevented from drawing a nut of nominal thread size 12.33 mm. For most standard items used in engineering (and bolts are no exception), there is a preferred range and it makes sound financial sense to select from it so as to avoid holding a lot of seldom-used items in stock. Even for specialized items which do not have a universally accepted range, it is common to design a range using some rational basis such as Renard numbers (BSI Publication PD 6481). In order to prevent the use of off-standard items, it is best to stick to the principle of 'one size, one block'.

ISO tolerance symbols

It is a widespread practice to use standard ISO tolerance symbols and tolerance frames to define geometric tolerances. It is not proposed to deal with the principles of geometric tolerances here; a good grounding can be obtained by reading BS 308 Part 3. A list of tolerance symbols is shown in

Appendix A. A tolerance frame is a box containing tolerance information which is of three kinds: the tolerance symbol, the tolerance value and an identification of the datum to which the tolerance applies. BS 308 defines standard proportions for tolerance symbols which are conveniently defined as blocks; you may have defined them already during the previous section. It also saves a good deal of time to define tolerance frames as blocks in which the tolerance symbols, tolerance values and datums can be written. There are several common layouts of tolerance frames (shown in Appendix A) and you can define and store each of these as a block. You will find that it saves time later if you are engaged in detail drafting.

Other standard marks used in drafting

Examples of other conventional drafting symbols are standard notes such as 'All dimensions in mm' and 'All unspecified blend radii 1 mm'. If there is a wide variety of standard notes, then it may be beneficial to define these as blocks.

PART NO	DESCRIPTION	NO OFF

Figure 13.4   Parts list

It also saves times if table headings for items such as part lists and issues lists are also kept as blocks – Figure 13.4 shows an example. Since it is not known beforehand how long these tables will be, or if they will be needed at all in the case of the parts lists, it is useful if they are stored as blocks. In each of these, lines can be added below the block for the items to be listed.

Among other symbols commonly used is the machining symbol. Not only does this indicate that a surface is to be machined, it can also be used to show surface texture and machining lay. A widely used layout is shown in Figure 13.5 and, again, drawing time can be saved by keeping machining symbols as blocks.

Other applications of blocks

A very common design constraint is that a particular component must fit inside some space envelope. A neat way of checking whether the component collides with the housing in which it is to fit is to draw the housing, to define the component as a block and then place the component in its working position. Points of possible collision can be examined in detail by zooming the drawing around the suspicious area. This is most useful when the component is mobile.

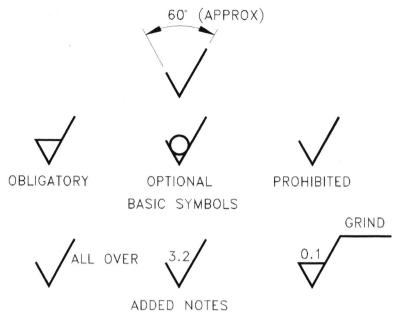

Figure 13.5 Machining symbols

A good example is in the design of workstations which are to be used by human beings. It is part of a designer's job to ensure that no human is affected adversely by the design, but it is a common experience to use a device, even occasionally an article of furniture, which causes discomfort. There are computer systems which can be used to aid ergonomic design but these are often unavailable to designers unless they work in a specialized field. The example which will be discussed next is a fairly crude attempt to use blocks to create a lay figure which can be used in the design of workstations such as tables and chairs.

Example. **Use of blocks to construct a lay figure**

Brief
Define blocks which will represent the different parts of a human body and which may be joined together and placed in various postures.

Plan of action
The body may conveniently be divided into:

A head, articulated at the neck.
A torso, articulated at the neck and pelvis.
Two upper arms, articulated at shoulder and elbow.
Two lower arms, articulated at elbow and wrist.
Two hands, articulated at the wrist.
Two upper legs, articulated at pelvis and knee.
Two lower legs, articulated at knee and ankle.
Two feet, articulated at the ankle.

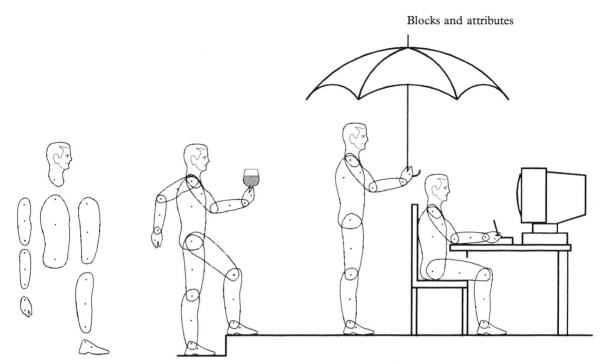

Figure 13.6   Example: Block for a human body

We need, then to define eight blocks. On each block, there are three characteristic points: the top one determines where it is joined to the body section above, the bottom one dictating its own angular position. The middle point is the position of its centre of gravity. A particular posture may be generated by positioning a body section and then inserting the other sections relative to it. The centre of gravity is used for designing objects like chairs.

Figure 13.6 is a fairly crude attempt at defining a lay figure. It is reasonably well proportioned for a male of average build. Several improvements could be made; for example, lines could be added at the joints to show maximum articulation; for a realistic system, it would be necessary to provide different models for different builds (or 'somatotypes'); a female figure would obviously have different proportions; the limbs of taller or shorter people are not in the same proportion to the torso as in those of average heights; age and infirmity affect the maximum angle of articulation and other views, for example front and top views, would also be needed.

It would take a good deal of time and research to develop a working system but it is hoped that the example shown demonstrates the power of AutoCAD blocks in problems of this kind.

The profiles of the body sections in Figure 13.6 were drawn as linear polylines and then smoothed using the **Spline curve** option in **PEDIT**. It is important that there should be as few line segments as possible without oversimplifying the forms to the point where they are unrecognizable. The detail on the face was added by using the **SKETCH** facility. It is completely unnecessary but we got carried away a little.

Introduction to attributes

In drafting applications such as jig and fixture design, it is common to use parts from a proprietary range of tooling aids. If a lot of this kind of work is to be done, it is beneficial to define the most frequently used components as blocks. This considerably reduces drawing time. Of course, the overhead of organizing the parts into blocks must be taken into account, but once this has been done the increase in drawing productivity can be remarkable. In many applications, the useful information about a component is not just graphical. AutoCAD permits textual information to be associated and stored with a block; the separate pieces of information are called 'attributes'. Attributes are useful in any application where a displayed object can have associated textual information.

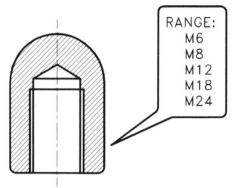

Figure 13.7   Domed nut

An example might be the range of domed nuts shown in Figure 13.7. Each nut in the range might be defined as a block so that it could be placed on a drawing without any actual drafting. We could also associate with each block the following information:

Part number
Description
Weight
Manufacturer's details
Cost

These attributes could be defined and stored at the time the block was defined. The attributes could be used to generate parts lists and other useful documentation. It would probably be convenient, in this case, to deal with the attributes in different ways. For example:

(a) The part number would probably be invariable – it would retain the same value each time the block was inserted. And each time the block was used, the part number could be written on the drawing in a fixed position relative to the graphical information.

(b) The part description might be variable if we wished to change from one language to another to suit the customer. It might not be considered desirable to clutter up the drawing by writing the description near the part – the attribute would be invisible. But it would be convenient to associate it with the block, so that parts lists could be generated automatically. The user would be prompted for the description on block insertion, but if none were provided, a default description would be assumed.

(c) The cost might be constant in the sense that the user would not be prompted for a value each time the block was inserted but it might be necessary, for some customers, to edit this attribute so as to provide an element of differential costing.

Attributes, then, can have three associated text strings:

- The attribute value is the actual information that is stored away for one particular instance of a block – e.g. 'Hutmutter'. This can be constant or variable, and, in the latter case, there might be a default value – 'Domed nut'.
- The attribute tag is the text describing its class. For example, the tag 'description' might be used to define the text class of which particular examples are: 'Domed-nut', 'Acorn-nut', 'Hutmutter' and 'Ecrou-borgne' (notice – no blanks). It acts somewhat like a string variable in a programming language.
- The attribute prompt is the text which will be output when the user is asked for the value of a variable attribute.

Attribute definition

Attributes are set up using the command sequence:

Command:**ATTDEF**
Attribute modes – Invisible:N Constant:N Verify:N Preset:N
Enter (ICVP) to change, RETURN when done.

The mode settings can be changed one by one; for example, the attribute can be made invisible by returning **I**. This acts as a toggle, the attribute could be returned to visibility by once more returning **I**. As each mode is set, the prompt is repeated, but with the settings changed. When **RETURN** is input to show that the setting is complete, the continuation depends on whether the attribute is constant or not.

For a constant attribute, neither attribute prompt nor default values are needed, so the command continues:

Attribute tag:
Attribute value:

For a non-constant attribute, the continuation is:

Attribute tag:
Attribute prompt:
Default attribute value:
Attribute value:

After the modes and text values have been satisfactorily specified, the text position, style, height and rotation angle are required. The prompt is the familiar text prompt:

Start point or Align/Centre/Fit/Middle/Right/Style:
Height <default>:
Rotation angle <default>:

The attribute tag is then displayed on the drawing and it is usual to position it somewhere near the graphics with which it will be associated. It is occasionally useful to use attributes as entities divorced from graphics. An example would be on a standard drafting sheet, where variable attributes could be used for the drawing title and other administrative information. The drafter could then be prompted for the information bit by bit, which would ensure that a standard text size and style were used. It would be possible to process these attributes to provide a drafting office management system.

The procedure is repeated for each attribute required. When this has been done, the graphics and the relevant attributes can be formed into a block by using the command **BLOCK**, and by creating a selection set containing the graphical entities and the attributes which have been displayed on the screen as their tags.

Example. Attribute definition

Brief
Define as blocks the domed nuts shown in Figures 13.7 and 13.8, the definition including the attributes described earlier.

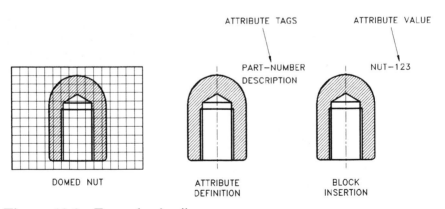

ATTRIBUTE TAGS   ATTRIBUTE VALUE

PART−NUMBER   NUT−123
DESCRIPTION

DOMED NUT   ATTRIBUTE DEFINITION   BLOCK INSERTION

Figure 13.8 Example: Attributes

Plan of action
The left hand component will be taken as representative. The nut is drawn, neglecting the text. The attributes Part Number and Description will be added, Part Number being constant, Description variable. The drawing and attributes will be defined as a block called DNUT1.

Command sequence
The following assumes that the nut has been drawn and the text style defined.

> Command:**ATTDEF**
> Attribute modes – Invisible:N Constant:N Verify:N Preset:N
> Enter (ICVP) to change, RETURN when done:**C**
> Attribute modes – Invisible:N Constant:Y Verify:N Preset:N
> Enter (ICVP) to change, RETURN when done:**RETURN**
> Attribute tag:**Part-Number**
> Attribute value:**NUT-123**
> Start point or Align/Centre/Fit/Middle/Right/Style:**Pick start point of text**

The attribute tag is now displayed at the point picked. The next attribute is defined.

> Command:**RETURN**
> Attribute modes – Invisible:N Constant:Y Verify:N Preset:N
> Enter (ICVP) to change, RETURN when done:**I**
> Attribute modes – Invisible:Y Constant:Y Verify:N Preset:N
> Enter (ICVP) to change, RETURN when done:**C**
> Attribute modes – Invisible:Y Constant:N Verify:N Preset:N
> Enter (ICVP) to change, RETURN when done:**RETURN**
> Attribute tag:**Description**
> Attribute prompt:**Description of part**
> Default attribute value:**DOME NUT**
> Start point or Align/Centre/Fit/Middle/Right/Style:**Specify start of text**

The block can now be defined and named; it will contain both graphics and attributes. In this case, if the tags have been placed conveniently, selection can be done by one window. Notice that although the Description attribute is invisible, the tag *is* displayed so that it can be selected. When the block has been defined, it is erased. This is a check that all graphics entities and attributes have been selected as part of the block.

The correctness of the procedure can be confirmed by inserting the defined block.

> Command:**INSERT**
> Block name (or ?):**DNUT1**
> Insertion point:**Pick a point**
> X scale factor<1>/Corner/XYZ:**RETURN**
> Y scale factor(default = X):**RETURN**
> Rotation angle<0.00>**RETURN**

So far, the normal **INSERT** command has been carried out. But this block contains attributes one of which is variable and its value must be filled in. What happens next is determined by whether or not you have the advanced user interface. If not, the command proceeds:

> Enter attribute values:Description of part **Hutmutter** Command:

Otherwise a dialogue box will be displayed. The attribute default is displayed and can be selected by hitting the OK button. If a new value is required, the pointer is moved to the appropriate strip, the value input, the verify button hit and the box left by hitting the OK button.

In either case, if the Verify mode was selected when the attribute was defined, the system will display the current value and you will be given a chance to change it, if it is in error.

Editing attributes

It is possible to edit existing attributes using the command **ATTEDIT**. Before doing this, it is useful to make all the attribute values visible, usually on a temporary basis. This is done using the command sequence:

Command:**ATTDISP**
Normal/On/Off<current value>:

N observes the mode setting of all attributes, **ON** makes them all visible and **OFF** makes them all invisible.

Attribute editing can be carried out on all the attributes on a drawing, on selected sets of attributes or on individual attributes. If editing of individual attributes is selected, then *all* the properties: position, text height, rotation angle, text style, layer and colour can be edited. Otherwise, only attribute values can be edited. Sets of attributes can be selected for edit by using the common wild card convention ('?' = any single character, '*' = a string of any number of characters). Editing of all attributes can be done by using the wild card '*'.

A typical case where global editing would be useful is in an electrical schematic of a standard device. One attribute might be the tolerance on resistors. Normally, 10% tolerance would be considered satisfactory and this would be the preset attribute value. However, the odd customer might have more stringent requirements and it would be convenient in those cases to edit the attribute value to '5%' on all the resistors in the device.

The command sequence for attribute editing is:

Command:**ATTEDIT**
Edit attributes one at a time?<Y>:**Specify either Y or N**

Whether **Y** or **N** is returned, the next action will be that specific sets of blocks, attribute tags or values may be selected. This is done by answering the prompts:

Block name specification<*>:
Attribute tag specification<*>:
Attribute value specification<*>:

Replying to each of these with **RETURN** will specify all eligible attributes. We could also specify, say, all the blocks DOM1, DOM2, . . . by entering the block name 'DOM*'.

Y results in individual editing. Particular attributes or sets of attributes may be specified by their block names, tags and values and then selected by pointing in the usual way. It must be remembered that only non-constant and preset attributes can be selected. It is, of course, necessary to have something to point at, and **ATTDISP** is used, if invisible attributes are to be edited. It also follows that, in order to be selected, attributes must be positioned on the current display. All properties of the identified attributes can be changed by responding, possibly repeatedly, to the prompt:

Value/Position/Height/Angle/Style/Layer/Colour/Next < N > :

These options should be self-explanatory, with the exception of **Next**, which is used to move on to the next selected editable attribute. The command is terminated either by entering **Next** when there are no more attributes to be edited, or, as usual, by **CTRL-C**.

N results in global editing. Sets of attribute values (all of them if necessary) can be changed. This applies not only to the displayed attributes, but also to all the attributes on the drawing. The prompts in this case are:

Global edit of attribute values.
Edit only attributes visible on screen? < Y >

If **N** is entered, then the drawing must be regenerated because of the edit. AutoCAD saves time by holding back the regeneration until after all the values have been edited. If **REGENAUTO** is **ON** (which we have recommended as standard practice) the regeneration will be carried out automatically. Otherwise, you must **REGEN** it.

If editing has been confined to visible attributes, then the set of attributes can be selected. The prompt for this is:

Select attributes:

– and selection is as described previously. Whether, or not, editing has been restricted to visible attributes, the continuation is:

String to change:
New string:

The only difference is that visible attribute editing can be done with the aid of the displayed block, while non-visible editing must be done on the text screen, which flips automatically.

If the advanced user interface is available, editing can be done using a dialogue box. This is initiated by the command **DDATTE**. A block is selected, its variable attributes are displayed and they can be changed one by one. All the blocks on a drawing can be edited successively by using **MULTIPLE DDATTE**. This is a convenient way of doing bulk edits, but because of the constraints on the dialogue box size, edited attributes are restricted to a length of 34 characters.

Exercises

1 It is common practice to show holes on components by their centrelines and explanatory notes such as:

O6 CSK AT 90 TO O12,
O6 DRILL THROUGH, or
O12 X 25 DEEP.

Design a system of blocks, using separate attributes for such features as hole diameter and hole depth, and other comments such as 'DEEP', 'THROUGH', 'CSK', 'C'BORE' and 'S'FACE'.

2   Design a block representing diagrammatically a room of your house. This need not be elaborate, a simple rectangle will serve. Each insertion is to have a visible attribute value which states the purpose of the room and each is to have an inventory of the electrical and electronic equipment which is sited in it. The inventory will consist of a list of invisible attribute values, of descriptions of the equipment, with a corresponding list of invisible attribute values of the serial numbers and cash values of the equipment. On insertion, some of these attributes may be null. An example might be:

Tag	Value
ROOM	FRONT ROOM
EQUIPDESC-1	HI-FI
EQUIPNO-1	1357ab
COST-1	625
EQUIPDESC-2	TELEVISION
EQUIPNO-2	RZ3684
COST-2	315
………	………
COST-6	854

Store the block using **WBLOCK**, it will be used in the next chapter.

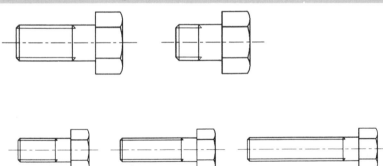

Figure 13.9   Exercise: BLOCK definition

3   Early in Chapter 3, it was stated that the side view of a bolt cannot be represented generally by a block because the threaded length is not in a constant ratio to the head geometry. Figure 13.9 demonstrates that this problem can be easily overcome, all the bolts shown being obtained from one block definition. Investigate this. (Hint: **EXPLODE** and **STRETCH** might come in handy).

14

Plotting and drawing files

A discussion of plotting hardware and how drawings are plotted in AutoCAD. Describes the different types of drawing file and how they are used. Commands covered include **PRPLOT**, **PLOT**, **SHELL**, **ATTEXT**, **DXFIN**, **DXFOUT**, **IGESIN** and **IGESOUT**.

Introduction to plotting equipment

An AutoCAD drawing file is a detailed record of the drawing. It can be stored on a floppy disk and held in a drawing register. The drawing can be retrieved and displayed on a graphics screen for discussion and reference. In concept, there is no reason why the drawing management should not be completely based on magnetic media with a computer controlled system for holding and issuing component drawings. It is, though, unusual to find such a system and the prime record is still predominantly the drawing plotted on pulp media.

Drawings can be plotted using either a specialized pen plotter or a printer which has a graphics capability. The printer-plotted drawing is normally used for checking and discussion purposes. Plotted drawings are of potentially higher quality and cost more; they are kept for 'best' – for record purposes.

Plotting with a printer plotter is straightforward. If the switch settings are right, the plot is automatic, rapid and of consistent quality. Most printers of the raster type – laser, inkjet and dot matrix – can produce a reasonably good plot. A typical printer-plotter, the Hewlett-Packard Laserjet, produces a plot at a maximum resolution of 300 dots per inch and so the picture is of a good quality. A difficulty is that the line thickness is as drawn; one cannot, for example, ensure that the profile of the component is drawn in lines bolder than those used for centrelines by using thicker pens. Also the plot size is restricted, often to A4 size.

Plotting with a pen plotter is a much more complex process and it is commonly noted that a good piece of engineering communication on the graphics screen is ruined by a bad plot. When, as seems inevitable, electrostatic plotters become cheaper, many plotting problems will be solved. Most installations still use pen plotters and a good deal of experimentation with media combinations is necessary to get the best results out of them. The main factors involved are the type of pen, the width of pen, the pen speed and the type of plotting paper. These are all interdependent.

Types of pen	Fibre tip Ceramic tip Ballpoint Pressurized ballwriter Liquid ink with steel, tungsten carbide or jewel tipped point pens
Pen widths	As was discussed earlier, the standard ISO range is: 0.13, 0.18, 0.25, 0.35, 0.5, 0.7, 1.0, 1.4 and 2.0 mm.
Pen speeds	Many plotters have adjustable pen speed which can be set by software. Even a typical cheap plotter has two speeds – 12.5 and 20 cm per second. AutoCAD can take advantage of this by giving users the capability of picking different speeds to suit different pens.
Paper types	The substance of a paper is measured in grams per square metre (gsm). The best plots can be obtained on special plot paper which is lint-free (so that it does not clog the pen) and of sufficient substance to support the pen action. The most common types are: Plotter paper (60–90 gsm) Tracing paper (90–100 gsm) Tracing vellum Matt drafting film

The combination chosen depends on the plotter and on the application. For example:

- Check plots can be done with pressurized ballwriters on lightweight plotter paper. They can be done at maximum plotter speed (100 cm per second, if the plotter permits) but no variation of line is possible – all lines are approximately 0.3 mm. In using the ink-pastes of pressurized ballwriters, some colours may be found to be more viscid than others.
- Precise plots can be done with tungsten carbide point pens using liquid opaque black ink on tracing paper of 90 gsm. The pen speed might be in the range 5 to 30 cm per second but this requires experimentation – if lines are too thick, the speed is too slow and vice versa.

If you have problems, you can get help from the plotter suppliers, but probably the best information comes from the providers of specialized plotter materials who will almost certainly have met your problem before.

Plotting in AutoCAD

In order to printer-plot a drawing, your printer should be connected to the normal printer port. AutoCAD should also be configured to suit the type of printer – the *AutoCAD Installation and Performance Guide* will tell you how. AutoCAD should also be configured for your plotter. If you have no spare port, the one used for your graphics input device can be shared: the devices are never in action together and the plot routine will give you an opportunity to switch.

A printer plot can be obtained by selecting either Option 4 from the Main Menu or the **PRPLOT** option which can be found in the **PLOT** item on the Screen Menu. A pen plot can be obtained by selecting either Option 3 from the Main Menu or the **PLOT** option which can be found in the **PLOT** item on the Screen Menu.

In initiating a plot from the Main Menu or from the Screen Menu, the difference is that the first option requires the name of a previously saved drawing file to be specified. The second option takes place inside the drawing editor and it is assumed that the drawing currently being edited is the one to be plotted so no name is necessary. Apart from this, the processes are identical.

The system now wants to know which part of the drawing is to be plotted. The prompt is:

Display, Extents, Limits, View or Window < D > :

'Display', in the case of the Main Menu command, means the display in force at the time of storage; details of this will have been stored with the drawing file. You may have noticed that a previously saved drawing, when retrieved, will be displayed in the same form it had when you saved it. In the case of the Screen Menu command, the picture shown at the **PLOT** or **PRPLOT** command will be taken.

'Extents' means the bounds of the entities drawn.

'Limits' means the whole drawing.

'View' means any named view that you have specified.

'Window' means that a defined portion of the drawing will be specified.

Apart from Extents, these options are not normally very useful when plots are called from the Main Menu, since they require coordinates which are not easily found without looking at the drawing. Since all are easily used from within the drawing editor, it is probably better to display the drawing first and accept the small overhead of time if you do not want to plot the whole drawing. A useful feature of plotting from the Main Menu is that it can be done from an alphanumeric display.

When the choice of the part of the drawing to be plotted has been made, the process continues by displaying the current plot specification. This might be something like:

Plot will NOT be written to a selected file
Sizes are in millimetres
Plot origin is at (0.00,0.00)
Plotting area is 817.00 wide by 570 high (A1 size)

Pen width is 0.25
Area fill will be adjusted for pen width
Hidden lines will NOT be removed
Plot will be scaled to fit available area
Do you want to change anything? <N>

These are some of the currently set specifications and if you are happy with them, type **RETURN** and the plot will carry on, with a pause for you to attend to the plotter. If you are using liquid ink pens, it is a good thing to test that the ink is flowing before proceeding. If the drawing is complicated and, for any reason, you want to stop the plot, just type **CTRL-C**. The plotter may carry on for a while since it holds a batch of plot commands in its internal buffer but, eventually, it will stop and you can return to the state you were in before you issued the command.

If you wish to change any of the specifications, AutoCAD will lead you through a dialogue which is quite detailed but easy to understand. The main characteristic which can be changed is the pen allocation.

There are conceptually fifteen pens in AutoCAD. Each of these is associated with a colour, with a linetype and with a pen speed. We can, then, show a particular linetype on the display in its own colour and use a separate pen width and appropriate speed when it is being plotted. The colours are the AutoCAD colour set, the linetypes are those provided by the plotter (not AutoCAD) while the pen speed setting is provided for plotters with a variable pen speed. The current settings are displayed – colour, pen number, linetype and pen speed for the fifteen possible pens:

Entity Color	Pen No.	Line Type	Pen Speed	Entity Color	Pen No.	Line Type	Pen Speed
1 (red)	1	0	36	9	1	0	36
2 (yellow)	1	0	36	10	1	0	36
3 (green)	1	0	36	11	1	0	36
4 (cyan)	1	0	36	12	1	0	36
5 (blue)	1	0	36	13	1	0	36
6 (magenta)	1	0	36	14	1	0	36
7 (white)	1	0	36	15	1	0	36
8	1	0	36				

Line types
0 = continuous line
1 = ...
2 = ---- ---- ---- ----
3 = ----- ----- ----- -----
4 = ------. ------. ------. ------.
5 = ---- - ---- - ---- - ---- -
6 = --- - - --- - - --- - - --- - -

Do you want to change any of the above parameters? <N>

If any of the pen characteristics needs to be changed, now is your chance to do it. If the quality of plots matters, it is advisable to prepare a plotter pen schedule.

Other characteristics are discussed in the following example.

Example. **Plotter Pen Schedule**

Brief
Prepare a pen schedule for drawings done with the prototype drawing
A4SHEET.

Plan of action
We shall assume that the plotter has the following characteristics:

4 pens
2 speeds
6 hardware linetypes
Liquid ink plotting pens

We shall also assume that, since the plotter has its own linetypes, these
will be used in preference to the AutoCAD versions. This will reduce plot
time but will necessitate all the non-continuous linetypes in the prototype
drawing being changed to continuous ones, otherwise the results will be
unpredictable. The hardware linetypes will be picked by using the allocated colour as key, so the layer allocation will remain the same
otherwise.

Since the sheet is A4, an appropriate pen set is 0.7 mm, 0.5 mm and
0.35 mm (Chapter 3). These will be placed in the pen carousel in positions 1, 2 and 3 respectively. The six hardware linetypes include equivalents of AutoCAD standard continuous, hidden, center and dot linetypes.
It is noted from the displayed plot specification that these are numbered
0, 2, 5 and 1.

Table 14.1   Layer schedule

Layer name	AutoCAD linetype	Colour	Purpose
SA4A	Continuous	White	Drafting sheet
SA4B	Continuous	Green	Drawing space
PART	Continuous	White	Component profile
HIDE	Hidden	Blue	Hidden detail
XHAT	Continuous	Green	Cross-hatching
CLNS	Center	Magenta	Centrelines
DIMN	Continuous	Green	Dimensions
NOTE	Continuous	Cyan	Text
NOTA	Continuous	Green	Text – small
CONS	Dot	Yellow	Construction lines

The layer schedule for A4SHEET described in Chapter 9 is shown in
Table 14.1. We have modified the original slightly by adding yet another
layer, NOTA, which will be used for smaller text. NOTE will be used for
the drawing title, number and any other large text. The reason for providing two text layers is not because the text is of a greater height but
because two different pen widths will be used. Now we can:

(a) Allocate the three pen widths to the linetypes, taking their purposes into account. This was discussed in Chapter 9.
(b) Allocate the pen widths to the two types of text. If the text heights are 7 mm and 5 mm, then the associated pen widths will be 0.7 mm and 0.5 mm (Chapter 9).
(c) Allocate pen speeds taking into account the pen widths. The widest pen (7 mm) will run at the top speed (36 cm/s), the other two pens will run at the slower speed of 18 cm/s.

The full pen schedule can now be written down (Table 14.2).

Table 14.2 Full pen schedule

Colour	Pen number	Hardware linetype	Pen speed
White	1	0	36
Green	3	0	18
White	1	0	36
Blue	2	2	18
Green	3	0	18
Magenta	3	5	18
Green	3	0	18
Cyan	2	0	18
Green	3	0	18
Yellow	3	1	18

The schedule in the example involves six pen allocations. The corresponding parameters can be changed:

Enter values. blank = Next value, Cn = Colour n, S = Show current values, X = Exit.

Entity Colour	Pen No.	Line-Type	Pen Speed	
1 (red)	1	0	36	Pen number<1>:**C2**
2 (yellow)	1	0	36	Pen number<1>:**3**
2 (yellow)	3	0	36	Linetype<0>:**1**
2 (yellow)	3	1	36	Pen speed<36>:**18**
3 (green)	1	0	36	etc.

. . . .

When the pen and linetype parameters settings are complete, the plot characteristics can be defined. These are:

Plot to file
Rather than plotting directly, the plot commands can be written to a file which can be processed by a program external to AutoCAD.

Size units
Some of the input that follows involves sizes of drawing and plot. These sizes can be specified in either inches or millimetres.

Plot origin
The plot defaults to an origin determined by the type of plotter. A pen plotter has its origin at the bottom left hand corner, a printer plotter at the top left. The origin can be set to some other point, the main reason for this being to plot more than one drawing on one piece of paper.

Plotting size
A list of all the plotting sizes supported on your plotter will be output. These will be the ISO or ANSI sizes with the maximum size (MAX) that the plotter can take. There may also be a non-standard size which is called USER. This is, as its name implies, user-specified. You can select a standard size from the list or, more rarely, define an off-standard size by specifying the sheet size in the standard units – in our case, millimetres.

Plot rotation
The plot can be rotated 90 degrees clockwise. Although most drawings match drafting sheets in that they are in landscape aspect ratio, occasionally it is more convenient to draw one in portrait aspect ratio (that is, with longer side vertical). If it were plotted that way, an over-sized drafting sheet would have to be used. This option plots the drawing sideways, which cures the problem.

Pen width
If your drawing contains solids or filled polylines, you can reduce the number of pen strokes taken for filling by providing the width of the pen used.

Area fill adjustment
In order to make filled areas accurate, the system can compensate for pen width and offset the boundaries of the areas by half one pen width in-wards. This only applies to pen plots.

Hidden line removal
This option is only used when three-dimensional work is being done. Since we are only concerned with two-dimensional drafting, you can ignore it.

Plot scale
The scale must be returned in the form: Plotted units = Drawing units. In our case, we are working in millimetres and usually this can be inter-preted as a direct scale. For example, if our drawing is too large to be drawn full size on the sheet that we have selected and needed to be scaled down by a scaling factor of 5, then we would define the scale as: **1 = 5**. Or, if we wished to scale up by a scaling factor of 5, then the scale definition would be **5 = 1**. It is possible to define the scale as **FIT** and the drawing will be scaled so that it fits the plotting paper, but this is bad drafting practice. For one thing, there is an ISO standard set of scales (Chapter 3). Also, if we are using a preprinted drafting sheet for the plot, as is common practice, it is possible that the drawing would overlap the title block.

AutoCAD will now confirm the plotting area and you can proceed with the plot. There will be a pause so that the pens can be loaded into the plotter and exercised, if they are of the liquid ink type. The plotting paper can be loaded and the plot initiated.

Drawing files

AutoCAD is a very useful tool for creating engineering drawings but, to exploit the full potential of computer aided design, it is best to regard the drafting system as a means of generating a component database. This means that the geometry and attributes that define a component are accessible to other programs. In order to communicate between programs successfully, the format in which information is held must be formally and consistently defined. AutoCAD can produce drawing data in several well-defined formats and so the drawing information that it generates is accessible for processing by external programs. There are many programs available that can feed off AutoCAD in this way.

The drawing files produced by AutoCAD – those with the extension .DWG – are held in a compacted form which is not easily accessible for external processing. Autodesk provide very little information about drawing file format and, in fact, the manual contains a disclaimer which states that the format is not guaranteed to be consistent from issue to issue. This does not spring from any desire to be secretive – AutoCAD is a much more open system than most others on the market – but to give some scope for development. There is fortunately another format different from that used by the drawing file, which is not so compact but is well-defined, and *is* highly suitable for use by external programs. This is the Drawing Interchange file (or DXF) format. DXF files have an extension of .DXF and exist in two versions, ASCII files, in which the information is stored in character form, and binary form, in which the information is held in a rather more compact format. Data in either of these two forms can be passed to other programs, for example:

- Component geometry can be passed to a computer aided manufacturing system so that the machining of the part can be simulated on the screen and cut files passed to a machine tool.
- Drawings can be passed to Desk Top Publishing systems to help in the preparation of technical documentation such as brochures.
- Attribute values can be processed to produce parts lists and bills of material.
- Text entities can be examined by a Drafting Management system and drawing numbers and issues lodged in a drawing register.

A common procedure is the extraction of attribute data from a drawing to produce parts lists and other documentation. As we have stated, this can be done by an external program acting on the DXF file. It is possible, in Auto-CAD, to extract attribute information from the drawing definition and store it in a file using commands inside the drawing editor. This is done by referring to a previously created file (a 'template' file) containing a definition of the information to be extracted and the form in which it is to be held. The extracted attribute data can be held in either variable length record form (CDF) or fixed length record form (SDF). The form chosen depends on the application for which the data will be used; as usual, variable length records are more compact, but require more processing time.

A slightly different case where communication between programs is used is in the passing of drawing information between one drafting system and another. The classic case is when a small firm supplies parts to a larger firm and the buyer insists that the component drawings are passed to them in a form that can be directly transferred into their computer aided design system. It is likely that the two systems are different and, if so, it is certain that the drawing file formats will be incompatible. The difficulty can be resolved in two ways: by developing a specialized translator program which will convert one format to the other, or by using an intermediate 'neutral' format. The first method will be efficient and clean but will be expensive since it will be necessary to write translator programs for every combination of drafting systems and, what is probably even more costly, to keep the translator programs up to date with developments in the drafting systems. The second method involves a two-stage translation process, the transmitting system's format to the neutral format and the neutral format to the receiving system's format, so is comparatively slow. But, if the vendors of each system provide the translation software as a useful facility, the user will have very little difficulty in transferring drawing information.

The most widely used neutral format is the Initial Graphics Exchange Specification (IGES) and AutoCAD, like many other systems, provides mechanisms for transmitting and receiving drawing files in IGES format. It must be admitted, however, that communication between systems is not quite as simple as we have implied here. In practice, since every system has its own idiosyncratic set of facilities, it is often necessary for the partners in the communication process to come to an agreement about the standard set of facilities which will be used. IGES files have the extension '.IGS'.

In summary:

- Drawing files are a compact method of storing drawings but are not easily processed by external programs. They have the extension '.DWG'.
- DXF files are less thrifty with store but are easily processed by external programs. They have the extension '.DXF'.
- IGES files are in a standard neutral format and are used for transferring drawing information between AutoCAD and other proprietary drafting systems. They have the extension '.IGS'.

It is interesting to compare the sizes of files. A simple benchmark drawing (Figure 14.1) was stored in various formats and the sizes of each were:

Drawing file:	TEST.DWG	9499 bytes
DXF file (binary):	TEST.DXF	6869 bytes
DXF file (ASCII):	TEST.DXF	11544 bytes
IGES file:	TEST.IGS	20090 bytes

This illustrates the penalty that must commonly be paid for standardization and also explains why AutoCAD drawings are stored in a non-standard, but compact, form.

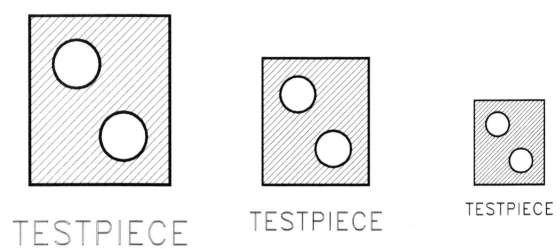

Figure 14.1 Benchmark drawing

Extracting attributes from drawing files

Before we can extract attribute information from a drawing, we must set up a template file. In this is defined the *type* of information required and the details of the *field* where it is to be stored. For example, in the block ROOM described in Exercise of Chapter 13, the attributes were:

ROOM-NAME
EQUIP-DES1
COST1
. . . .
. . . .
EQUIP-DES4
COST4

If we wished to extract the ROOM-NAME and COST1, COST2, COST3 and COST4 attributes, then the template would contain the attributes tags and descriptors of the fields in which the values were to be held. In this case, a suitable template might be:

ROOM-NAME   C020000
COST1   N010002
COST2   N010002
COST3   N010002
COST4   N010002

The field descriptor appended to each tag is of a rigorous format. The letter 'C' or 'N' defines the type of attribute value, either 'character' or 'numeric'. The following three digits specify the total field length in character positions. The last three digits are only relevant to numeric values and specify the number of decimal places that the stored number is to have. For instance, the COST1 attribute value is to be extracted and stored over ten character positions. It is to have two decimal places. The field width will have space for a possible sign, six digits for the whole number part, a decimal point and two digits for the fractional part. Thus the largest number that can be held is 999999.99.

Other information can be extracted from a block, for example, its name and the coordinates of its insertion point. These are specified by a code-name and a field length. The most useful are:

```
BL:NAME    Cwww000
BL:X       Nwwwddd
BL:Y       Nwwwddd
```

where the code-name is distinguished from an attribute tag by being prefixed by 'BL:' and the field descriptor is 'www', the field width, and 'ddd', the number of decimal points.

The template file is created using a text editor or word processor. Since it is a short and uncomplicated piece of text, the text editor EDLIN supplied with MS-DOS is quite adequate. It can be run easily from the drawing editor using the **SHELL** command, which permits us to use a single operating system command from within AutoCAD.

Command:**SHELL**

The screen then flips to the alphanumeric display and we continue:

DOS Command:**EDLIN INVENT.TXT**
*I

```
    1:*ROOM-NAME   C020000
    2:*COST1       N010002
    3:*COST3       N010002
    4:*COST4       N010002
    5:*CTRL-C
```
*E

If a template is available, the drawing from which extraction is to be made must be current in the drawing editor. The extraction is carried out by the command sequence:

Command:**ATTEXT**
CDF, SDF or DXF Attribute extract (or Entities)?<C>

If **Entities** is selected, separate entities can be picked for extraction. The prompt is then repeated so that the file type can be specified.

- CDF, the variable field length format has fields separated by commas. Character fields are enclosed in quotes and the format is much like that in the DATA statement in BASIC. In this format, specified field lengths are maxima.
- SDF is the fixed field length format. Fields have no separators but have a specified width.
- DXF is a format like the standard DXF which will be discussed later, but it is specialized to attribute extraction.

When the file type has been chosen, the command continues:

Template file <default>:

The name of the previously created template file should be input without extension since the system automatically adds '.TXT'.

Finally, the name of the file in which the extracted information is to be held is supplied:

Extract filename < drawing file > :

If we wish to extract the attributes defined in the file INVENT.TXT that we created earlier and hold them in fixed length record format in a file called ROOM_INV.TXT, the procedure will be:

Command:**ATTEXT**
CDF, SDF or DXF Attribute extract (or Entities)?< C >**S**
Template file < default >:**INVENT**
Extract filename:< HOUSE >:**ROOM_INV**
Command:

DXF files

A DXF file can be created from the drawing editor by the command sequence:

Command:**DXFOUT**
Filename < default >:**Enter filename – no extension**
Enter decimal places of accuracy (0 to 16)/Entities/Binary < 6 >:

As was mentioned earlier, there are two forms of DFX file, ASCII and Binary. ASCII is the default and holds numbers to a precision which must be specified. If Binary is selected, all numbers are held to the maximum precision of the computer and no decimal place specification is necessary. Entities allows objects to be individually placed in a DFX file. If this option is selected, the objects will be gathered into a selection set and the prompt is repeated so that the type of DFX file can be chosen. The file will be set up with an extension of '.DFX'.

A DFX file can be input to an empty drawing by the command:

Command:**DXFIN**:
Filename:

The format of a DXF file is a precise definition of all the settings and entities in the drawing. It consists of five sections:

- Header section. This contains a list of the statuses of over a hundred variables associated with the drawing. Examples are:
  $CLAYER   Current layer name
  $TEXTSTYLE   Current text style name
- Tables section. This contains definitions of items with names, for instance, linetypes and layers.
- Blocks section. This contains definitions of the entities that make up the blocks used in the drawing. Segregating these entities in this way means that only one detailed definition of a block is carried.
- Entities section. Details of all the drawing entities are held here. Note that

the block details have already been defined in the blocks section so only insertion point and similar details are carried in this section.

- End of file.

Because the format of DXF files is formally stated and rigorously ordered, it is not difficult to extract entity information from them. It is also possible to extract attribute information easily. Each entity is represented by a set of groups, each group taking up two lines in the file: a group code and a group value. The group code is a numeric value which defines the meaning of the group value. For example,

```
0          {Group code – start of entity definition}
LINE       {Group value – LINE entity}
10         {Group code – X coord of start point}
25.364     {Group value – X coordinate}
20         {Group code – Y coord of state point}
30.123     {Group value – Y coordinate}
......
......
```

IGES files

IGES files are easily created and input by using the commands **IGESOUT** and **IGESIN**. They, like DXF files, consist of five sections:

- Start section: Documentary details.
- Global section: Information to set up the drawing – for instance, units and scale.
- Directory section: List of entities which make up the drawing with pointers to their coordinates which are detailed in the next section.
- Parameter data section: Actual coordinates and text.
- Terminate section: Signals the end of the file.

An IGES drawing file is much larger than a DXF file of the same drawing. This is because of the necessary generality of the format which must be capable of defining drawings from many systems.

Exercises

1   Prepare a simple drawing. Convert it to DXF form and then read it back again.

2   Repeat Exercise 1 using the IGES format. Don't forget to keep the drawing *very* simple if storage is tight.

3   Perform your own benchmark test with a drawing not more complex than Figure 14.1.

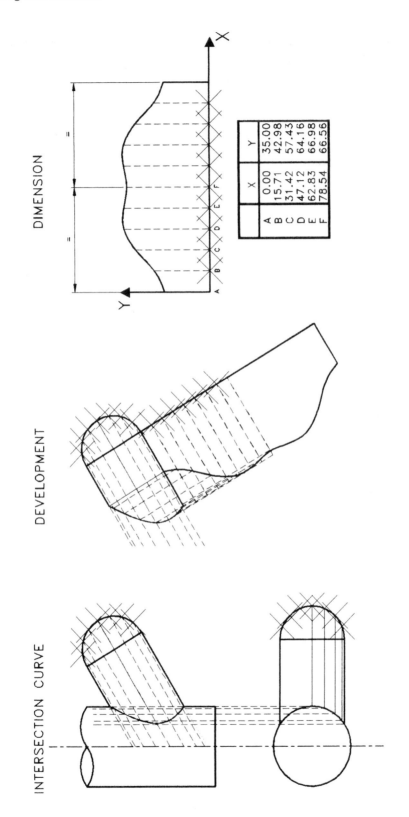

DIMENSION

	X	Y
A	0.00	35.00
B	15.71	42.98
C	31.42	57.43
D	47.12	64.16
E	62.83	66.98
F	78.54	66.56

DEVELOPMENT

INTERSECTION CURVE

Figure 14.2 Exercise: Developed form

4   Finally, a harder exercise to test your mastery of AutoCAD. Find and dimension the developed form of a cylinder which intersects another cylinder at an angle as shown in Figure 14.2. This may need **DIVIDE, ROTATE, LIST, POLYLINE, PEDIT** etc. The dimensions shown in the figure are approximate since they are taken from a splined polyline. When you are satisfied with the result, plot it to scale on fairly substantial paper, cut out the developed form and a rectangle which will wrap to become the intersected cylinder. Confirm the correctness of your developed form by testing whether the two shapes fit together.

Appendix A

Drafting conventions

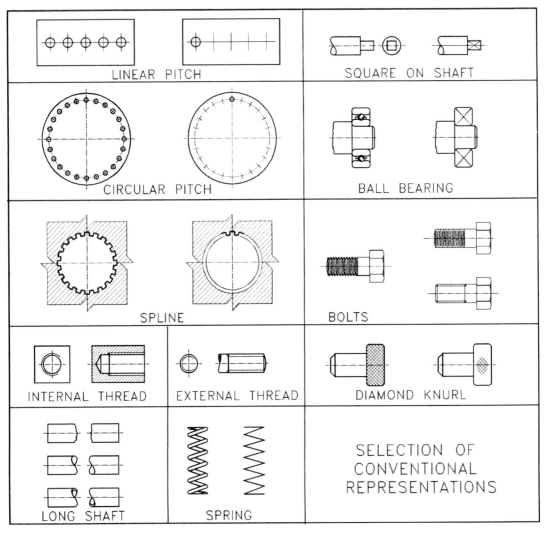

LINEAR PITCH

SQUARE ON SHAFT

CIRCULAR PITCH

BALL BEARING

SPLINE

BOLTS

INTERNAL THREAD

EXTERNAL THREAD

DIAMOND KNURL

LONG SHAFT

SPRING

SELECTION OF CONVENTIONAL REPRESENTATIONS

Tolerance frames and symbols

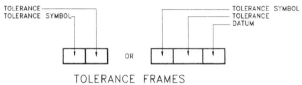

TOLERANCE FRAMES

SYMBOL	CHARACTERISTIC TOLERANCE
—	STRAIGHTNESS
//	PARALLELISM
○	ROUNDNESS
⌀	CYLINDRICITY
⌒	PROFILE OF A LINE
⌓	PROFILE OF A SURFACE
⊥	SQUARENESS
∠	ANGULARITY
↗	RUNOUT
⊕	POSITION
◎	CONCENTRICITY
≡	SYMMETRY
▱	FLATNESS

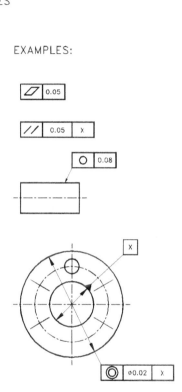

EXAMPLES:

Standard abbreviations (Table A1)

Table A1   A selection of drafting abbreviations

Abbreviation	Meaning
A/C	Across corners
A/F	Across flats
ASSY	Assembly
CHAM	Chamfer
CL	Centreline
CRS	Centres
C'BORE	Counterbore
C'SK	Countersink
CYL	Cylinder
DIA or Ø	Diameter
DRG	Drawing
FIM	Full indicated movement
LH	Left hand
LG	Long
MAX	Maximum
MIN	Minimum
MMC	Maximum metal condition
NO	Number
NTS	Not to scale
PCD	Pitch circle diameter
R	Radius
RH	Right hand
SH	Sheet
Sphere Ø	Spherical diameter
Sphere R	Spherical radius
S'FACE	Spotface
SQ	Square
STD	Standard
SWG	Standard wire gauge
TPI	Threads per inch
U'CUT	Undercut

Appendix B

AutoCAD commands

Command	Main menu item	Page no.
Aligned	DIM:	128
Angular	DIM:	135
Aperture	SETTINGS	148
Arc	DRAW	55–77
Area	INQUIRY	89, 90
Array	EDIT	85
Attdef	BLOCKS	171, 172
Attdisp	DISPLAY	174, 175
Attedit	EDIT	174
Attext	UTILITY	187
Axis	SETTINGS	47
Base	BLOCKS	164
Baseline	DIM:	128
Blipmode	SETTINGS	35
Block	BLOCKS	160, 161
Break	EDIT	81, 82
Chamfer	EDIT	69, 70
Change	EDIT	87, 88
Circle	DRAW	54, 55
Continued	DIM:	128
Copy	EDIT	71
Diameter	DIM:	134
Dim	DIM:	125–9, 134, 135, 138–41
Dim1	DIM:	125
Dist	INQUIRY	89
Divide	EDIT	88
Donut	DRAW	146
Dragmode	SETTINGS	163
Dtext	DRAW	109, 110
DXFin	UTILITY	188

Command	Main menu item	Page no.
Save	SAVE:	20
Select	EDIT	64–6
Setvar	SETTINGS	35
Shell	UTILITY	187
Sketch	DRAW	156, 157
Snap	SETTINGS	43, 45, 46, 152
Solid	DRAW	61, 62
Stretch	EDIT	84, 85
Style	SETTINGS	108
Text	DRAW	109
Trim	EDIT	82, 83
U	★★★★	53
UCS	UCS:	33, 36, 37
UCSicon	SETTINGS	33, 37
Undo	EDIT	66
Units	SETTINGS	36
Vertical	DIM:	127, 128
Vports	DISPLAY	41
View	DISPLAY	40
Viewres	DISPLAY	36
Wblock	BLOCKS	160–2
Zoom	DISPLAY	37–39

Useful AutoCAD system variables

AFLAGS	Attribute information.
APERTURE	OSNAP aperture box size.
AREA	Result of INQUIRY.
ATTMODE	Attribute visible or not.
AUNITS	Angular units.
AUPREC	Angular precision.
AXISMODE	Axis ON or OFF.
AXISUNIT	Space between ticks.
BLIPMODE	Blips ON or OFF.
COORDS	Coord read-out continuous or not.
DIMASO	Associative dimensioning ON or OFF.
DIMASZ	Arrow size.
DIMCEN	Centre mark size.
DIMDLI	Increment size for BASELINE.
DIMEXE	Overlap above dimension line.
DIMEXO	Gap on witness line.
DIMLIM	Generate limits or not.
DIMOXD	No external dimension lines.
DIMPOST	Default suffix for dimension text.
DIMRND	Rounding for text.
DIMSCALE	Scales dimension.

DIMSEI	First extension line present or not.
DIMSE2	Second extension line present or not.
DIMSHO	Immediate update or not.
DIMTAD	Text above dimension line or not.
DIMTIH	Text horizontal inside dimension lines.
DIMTIX	Text forced between dimension lines.
DIMTOFL	Dimension lines forced between extensions.
DIMTOH	Text horizontal outside dimension lines.
DIMTOL	Tolerance generation.
DIMTP	Positive tolerance.
DIMTSZ	Tick size.
DIMTVP	Text above or below dimension line.
DIMTXT	Dimension text size.
DMTM	Negative tolerances.
DRAGMODE	Entities dragged during edit or not.
DWGNAME	Drawing name.
FILLETRAD	Fillet radius.
FILLMODE	Polylines and solids filled or not.
GRIDMODE	Grid ON or OFF.
GRIDUNIT	Pitches of grid.
LIMCHECK	Limit check ON or OFF.
LIMMAX	Upper right of drawing limits.
LIMMIN	Lower left of drawing limits.
LTSCALE	Linetype scale factor.
MIRRTEXT	Mirrored text backwards or forwards.
ORTHOMODE	Toggle for ORTHO.
OSMODE	Values for OSNAP nodes.
PDMODE	Type of point pattern.
PDSIZE	Size of point pattern.
PICKBOX	Selection box size.
QTEXTMODE	Qtext ON or OFF.
REGENMODE	Regeneration automatic or not.
SKETCHING	Sketch increment.
SKPOLY	Sketch in lines or polylines.
SNAPANG	Current angle of grid.
SNAPBASE	Current origin of grid.
SNAPISOPAIR	Current isoplane.
SNAPMODE	Snap toggle.
SNAPSTYL	Normal or isometric snap.
SNAPUNIT	Snap spacing.
SPLINESEGS	Line segments per spline.
SPLINETYPE	Quadratic or cubic B-splines.
TEXTSIZE	Current size of text.
TEXTSTYLE	Name of current text style.
UCSICON	UCS icon ON or OFF.
UCSNAME	Current UCS name.
UCSORG	Current UCS origin.

Index